Why be Jewish?

Why be Jewish?

A Guide for Discovering and Maintaining Jewish Traditions and Values

RICHARD D. BANK

JASON ARONSON INC.
Northvale, New Jersey
Jerusalem

This book was set in 11 pt. Rockwell by Alabama Book Composition of Deatsville, AL.

10 9 8 7 6 5 4 3 2 1

Library of Congress Cataloging-in-Publication Data

Bank, Richard D., 1947–
     Why be Jewish and how to do it / Richard D. Bank.
          p.   cm.
     Includes index.
     ISBN 0-7657-6169-6
          1 Judaism—Essence, genius, nature.   2. Jews—Identity.   3. Judaism—
     United States.   4. Judaism—20th century.   I. Title.
     BM565 .B27 2002
     296.7—dc21
                                                              00–056941

Printed in the United States of America on acid-free paper. For information and catalog, write to Jason Aronson Inc., 230 Livingston Street, Northvale, NJ 07647-1726, or visit our website: www.aronson.com

To my parents, Ruth and Louis Bank,
who afforded me my Jewish identity.

To my wife, Francine,
with whom I have shared our Jewish identity.

To my sons, Cory and Ari,
who will experience their own Jewish identity.

Acknowledgment

While considering alternatives for my next book length project, my agent asked me a heavily laden question. "Richard," she said, "What do you want to do with the rest of your life?" It took but an instant for me to decide. The answer became this book.

For her keen insight which resulted in the birth of this book, and her steadfast support along the way, I am deeply grateful to Carol Susan Roth.

Contents

Introduction

Throughout the American Jewish Community, hands of all sorts are wringing—wizened rabbis, presidents of Jewish federations and organizations, parents of children who plan to marry non-Jewish spouses, and people like you and me—nontraditional and unaffiliated Jews—we are all asking the same question, "What to do? What to do?" How do we avoid becoming, as the title of Alan Dershowitz's book suggests, "The Vanishing American Jew"?

Of course, this supposes another question raging beneath the surface which few of us have dared to even utter: "Why be Jewish in the first place?" And yet, despite even this, our Jewish identity is still important to most of us. Even though it may just be a gut feeling gnawing away in our *kishkes* saying there is something sad about our progeny in the not-too-distant future placing gifts under Christmas trees, or not having a clue about the way matzo laid in our bellies like lead, nor knowing why we would slap our foreheads grimacing an "*oy veh*," nor realizing how the murder of six million Jews in the Holocaust is more than history for us but something that sears our souls because it was *our people* who perished in the ovens.

This sense of loss was brought home to me in a very unusual way not long ago. In fact, I wrote about it and it was published in *Jewish Currents*. I would like to share this with you now.

L'Shanah Tovah in the Canadian Rockies

My wife, Francine, and I do not consider ourselves ethnocentric people. In fact, we take pride in our belief in the oneness of humanity. That aside, however, what do you suppose was the first thing we did when receiving the list of our fellow travelers scheduled to undertake a group hike in the Canadian Rockies right after Labor Day? Why, we checked to see what names sounded Jewish of course.

Because the trekkers hailed from all parts of the country as well as South America and only twenty people were in the group, we didn't expect other Jews. Not that this mattered, but we were curious. So it came as some surprise when, perusing the roster, I detected other landsleit. David and Bonnie Jacobs from New York, and fellow Manhattanites Barbara Schlesinger and Brenda Cohen (surnames have been changed but still reflect their ethnic nature), were giveaways, as was Jessica Schwartz from Connecticut. Stuart Gold, who was paired with Denise Hallahan, was questionable, but since he hailed from L.A., I suspected he might fit the bill. There were other possibilities, and it was beginning to look like we were heading for the Catskills rather than the Rockies. Yet, what lay ahead was most unexpected and would leave a scene in my mind that I will remember for some time.

On the bus transporting us from Calgary to Yoho National Park for our first day of hiking, I sat across the aisle from Mariana and Thomas Frank, who were from Brazil. My ears perked when they indicated they spoke several languages including German. "Frank" could be German Jewish or Gentile and the fact that so many Nazis had obtained refuge in Brazil was not lost on me. Thomas had a guarded demeanor about him. Was it because it was the first day among strangers or was there something to hide in his family's past? I was determined to find out.

The next day, climbing Mt. Stephan, I learned from Barbara, who claimed she had a knack for unearthing personal information about people, that Mariana's mother was born Jewish but converted. Whenever possible, as we moved along the trail, I tried catching a phrase or intonation to give me a clue about Thomas, but there was nothing. That night at dinner, I made it my business to sit at their table.

Someone said they admired Thomas and Mariana for possessing such a faculty for languages. This was my opening. I mentioned that I grew up speaking English and German, since my grandparents came to live with us after their liberation from the camps. I watched Thomas very carefully as I said this. The slightest blush on his face and I was ready to pounce. But instead, it was Mariana who leaned toward me.

"Which camp?" she asked.

"Theresienstadt," I replied.

"My mother survived Auschwitz," Mariana said, locking her eyes onto mine in silent acknowledgment that we shared the history of the Holocaust.

"Then you're Jewish?" I asked, beginning to doubt Barbara's reliability as a source of information.

"Yes, but we don't do much about it," answered Mariana. I turned to Thomas. My stare demanded some answer.

"My father left Germany in 1935," Thomas said. "His father was able to leave in 1939. A day later he would not have made it out. The rest of the family was murdered."

So much for "Boys in Brazil," I thought. There was much I wanted to share with Thomas and Mariana, but before I could, I was interrupted by Philip Fedous, who looked and spoke like Robert Redford and was seated to my right.

"Some of my grandmother's family died in Dachau," said Phil.

"Why?" I asked, thinking they might have been political prisoners.

"Because they were Jewish," he answered. I was floored. Seeing the look of astonishment on my face, Phil went on.

"It's a very interesting story," he began. "I never knew my grandmother was Jewish until she was in her eighties. She came to America and moved to California in 1906, where she met and married my grandfather, who was a Lebanese Christian. My mother and her sisters were raised Christian."

"So how did you find out she was Jewish?" I asked.

"Twenty years ago, I was planning a trip to Europe. When my grandmother heard I was going to Germany, she said she might have relatives there. All I had were some names and her guess that they were living in a town outside Frankfurt. To make a long story short, I located them. That's when I learned her sisters died in Dachau but their children had survived. They remained in Germany, married, and had families."

"And they maintained their Jewish identity?"

"Yup. My Jewish cousins made a special point of inviting me for a Friday night dinner, setting white cloth over the table, lighting candles, and blessing the wine and bread. That's when I realized I was one-quarter Jewish. The next year, I took my grandmother back to visit the family she had left behind seven decades before."

Phil took another sip of wine, and poured some more for each of us from one of the bottles we were sharing. Phil Fedous—a French name, Arab and Christian heritage, Robert Redford look-alike, and Jewish blood flowing in his veins! In fact, according to Orthodox tradition, since the bloodline was maternal, Phil was still a Jew. Who would have figured? But the biggest surprise awaited me the next day.

One thing about hiking is that you make every rest room stop you can. I was on my way back from such a respite when I picked up the middle of a conversation between Bonnie Jacobs and one of our guides, Sheryl DeLeo. Sheryl was this spunky young lady, always encouraging us, and a pleasure to be with. Bonnie had just finished explaining that when her kids were little, they used to celebrate Christmas until, one day, her oldest son protested that they were Jewish and Jews don't celebrate that holiday. Though Bonnie did not see anything religious about Christmas, she acquiesced. Her husband David added that their four grown children were all very active in temple, and the boy who had once admonished them about Christmas had recently pledged an endowment to ensure the continued existence of Hillel at his alma mater.

"So what does all this have to do with Sheryl?" I whispered to my wife, but not low enough that Sheryl hadn't overheard.

"I'm Jewish," Sheryl said to me, matter-of-factly. "And we were talking about my family celebrating Christmas." Our guide out here in the middle of nowhere is a Jew? As I strapped on my backpack, I was beginning to think we were like the Hebrews embarking on a journey led by a female Moses.

The next day, I kept pace with Sheryl, or, more likely, she slowed down for me. In any event, I wanted to know more about this Jewish mountaineer.

"Are both your parents Jewish?" I asked.

"Yes. My babba came over from Russia. It was like 'Fiddler on the Roof.' She and her family first went to the States but eventually made their way to Toronto. My father's father was a Bolshevik and a Trotskyite. When things got uncomfortable in Russia, he came to Canada."

*Sheryl went on telling stories about sumptuous holiday din-
ners and her bubbe (which she kept pronouncing "babba") and
zeyda. She married an Italian, and while I never learned for certain
whether her children were being raised as Catholics, I knew they
were not taught anything about being Jewish. And again, I considered, according to Orthodox halakhah, her son and daughter are
Jews.*

*That was our last day of hiking. The next morning, we said our
good-byes to the guides and boarded the bus. As I was standing
around, Bonnie went over to Sheryl, who had her two children in
tow. They were adorable kids—the boy about five and the girl
maybe eight, and both had brown hair and freckles like their
mother.*

*Bonnie gave Sheryl a warm hug and wished her a happy
New Year. Sheryl knitted her eyebrows, regarding Bonnie with a
confused gaze. "It's Rosh Hashanah next week," Bonnie clarified.
Sheryl cocked her head in vague acknowledgment.*

*As the bus was pulling away, I peered back at Sheryl, stand-
ing on her toes with a big smile on her face, waving at us, and one
kid on each side of her. As she began to fade in the distance, I
thought of Phil's grandmother, whom he hadn't known to be Jewish
until she neared the end of her life, and it seemed to me that Sheryl
was destined to share the same fate. Somewhere, in the remote
background of progeny yet to be born, Sheryl will be the Jewish
grandmother.*

*Much has been said concerning the danger of Jews living
outside Israel losing their Jewish identity. I've read a great deal on
the subject and have written about it. Yet it has always been in the
abstract—happening to future generations. But in the Canadian
Rockies of all places, it had revealed itself in a group of a dozen
people drawn from all over the hemisphere and from different
walks of life.*

*I considered Phil in front of me. I glanced at Thomas and
Mariana, knowing the chances were their grandchildren would not
be Jews. I turned back, still able to see Sheryl waving with her son
and daughter. The sense of loss was heavy, because it became
very personal. These people and I had shared something special—whether experiences of the Shoah, or flights from pogroms,
or fat-laden meals our bubbas concocted. The days of such belonging were numbered and our children may be denied this.*

What to do? Answers abound, although I have not yet found

*any to be wholly satisfactory. Perhaps there is only one answer.
And that is what I learned the week before the Jewish New Year as
I ended a hiking trip in the Canadian Rockies.*

*It was all said in that moment when Bonnie Jacobs put her
arms around Sheryl, gave her a hug and a warm-hearted smile,
and wished her Shana Tovah. Perhaps that is all any of us can do.
Not berate each other or find fault. It won't do any good. Just a hug
and a smile and hope that maybe it will be enough to strengthen
the bond among us as Jews.*

I have a name for people like Sheryl and Thomas and Mariana.
I call them "invisible Jews." The appellation came to me recently
when a young man, an attorney to whom I was referring a case, met
with me in my office. He had blond hair, was tall and attired in a
conservative suit and white shirt, and was carrying a worn brown
leather brief case. His name was generic. I'll call him John Thomas
and John was soft spoken and very polite. We talked for almost half
an hour and just as we were about to part, he asked me if I was
working on another book. I didn't really want to go into the subject
since I knew it would hold no interest for him so I quickly mumbled it
was about Jewish identity.

That's when John blurted, "Boy, is that a book I can use!"

I was floored. "You're Jewish?" I asked and John nodded in the
affirmative.

It turned out John used his middle name because he hated his
last name of "Smith" which had been assigned to his grandmother at
Ellis Island. After John left, I realized that I had been blind to anything
Jewish about him. And that's when I grasped the fact that there are
hundreds of thousands of "invisible Jews" whom we will never even
recognize because names won't matter (with intermarriages soaring), our appearances blend in with our society, and we have no
accents or distinguishable demeanor.

In any event, I can't help but feel a sadness that there will be
fewer and fewer Jews in this country—that my great grandchildren
may have no more than an inkling there is thousands of years of
Jewish heritage in the blood coursing through their veins. I suppose
that at some time or another you also have felt this way or you

wouldn't have picked up this book. What is more, you are correct in your estimation of this impending loss.

The situation is serious. If current population trends continue and forecasts are even close on target, it is not unlikely that the American Jew will be placed on the endangered species list. The most optimistic predictions see barely five million American Jews in the year 2025 while some soothsayers auger that fifty years from now, Jews in the United States will have all but disappeared. Whether these are cries of alarmists or legitimate wake-up calls, a problem does exist.

The fact is that in absolute numbers, there are fewer Americans identifying themselves as Jews today than a half century ago. While the general population has more than doubled in the United States since World War II, the Jewish population has decreased slightly and, instead of representing over four percent of the country's populace, Jews comprise only 2.3 percent at the turn of the millennium. Moreover, given a lower than average birth rate and an intermarriage rate of fifty percent (as high as eighty percent in some areas if the Orthodox are removed from the equation), and with only one in four children of such marriages raised Jewish, the question is not "if" the Jewish population in the United States will continue to decrease but rather by "how much."

Oddly enough, the only projection showing an increase in the Jewish population assumes that the intermarriage rate will continue at fifty percent or more but the majority of children of these unions are raised Jewish. We'll return to this issue in Chapter 43.

What is also clear is that, regardless how many Jews there may be, we will become not only less recognizable amongst ourselves but practically indiscernible in American society. It is conceivable that the only distinguishable Jews will resemble the Amish, a sect living in closed communities cut off from society. This is because the one portion of the Jewish population which has gone against the current trend has been the Orthodox.

There are a number of reasons for this, not the least of which is their adherence to the command—"Be fruitful and multiply." With a negligible intermarriage rate, it is very possible that unless current projections are reversed, the only Jews left in the United States by the middle of the next century will be the Orthodox. While I certainly have no objection to a strong Orthodox Jewish presence, I would deeply regret the absence of other segments of the Jewish community.

If things are to change, it is up to people like you and me to do something about it. And although you may feel you're the oddball Jew because you don't belong to a synagogue, you are very mistaken. The fact is more than half of the Jews living in the United States are unaffiliated with any Jewish organization or synagogue. Add those Jews who are members of Jewish groups in name only or for whom synagogue is a two or three day a year event, and as many as two thirds of this country's Jews are not actively involved with a synagogue or Jewish institution to reinforce their Jewish identity.

So, if you still care about being a Jew—and we will soon address the question "Why be Jewish?"—and you want future generations to continue to be Jews because you think this is important for them and that the world may be a better place for it, the time has come to do something. Thus, we return to the quandary, "What to do? What to do?"

But first, how about we look and see what hasn't worked and isn't working for people like us. While guilt has always been a formidable weapon bludgeoning away at one's Jewish conscience, the cajoling, badgering, and berating that comes along with it isn't likely to be nearly as effective on an enlightened twenty-first century mind as it was in the past. Nor are those like you and me likely to be swayed by being denounced as "apikoros" (heretic), for not affiliating with one of the traditional branches of organized Judaism. The bottom line is that observing religious halakhah, either in whole or in part, is anathema to millions of American Jews. We just don't and won't buy into it.

Of course, one can say Jewish identity may be maintained apart from religion. We are a "people"—a "race"—with our very own country, Israel. But this begs the question. While Israel may be an important component of our Jewishness (Chapter 30), it cannot be the entire picture because then it would naturally follow that we should all board that hefty El Al plane with the kosher meals and abusive attendants and make aliyah. The thing is, almost all of us, even the Orthodox, consider the United States our home. So hanging our hats on Israel's mantle won't do the job.

What does this leave us? According to Queens College Professor Samuel Heilman in his book, *Portrait of American Jews*, "Jews have two choices at the end of the twentieth century—to be indistinguishable from other Americans or put themselves at odds with America." Well, excuse me Professor Heilman, but the "Jew" in me says when faced with two unacceptable choices, my "stiff neck" twists and turns for a third option. So here goes.

Several years ago, I was assigned to review a book by Yossi Klein Halevi who was born and raised an orthodox Jew in New York and for a time was a follower of Rabbi Meir Kahane. After a time, he began a process questioning the basic premises of his life and moved to Israel. His story, *Memoirs of a Jewish Extremist*, poses the issue this way: "I had long felt that some drastically new form of Judaism, strange and unexpected, must emerge from our experience in this century." Thinking about that, I looked back over our 4000 year history and I observed that ours has been a mutable existence.

Clearly, the Hebrews during the time of the patriarch Abraham had little in common with the Hebrews worshipping and sacrificing in Jerusalem at the Temple King David built who, in turn, bear slight similarity to the Israelites cast into the Diaspora after the destruction of the Second Temple. Nor was there much in common between those Jews and their descendants of later times who studied in small shuls and centers of learning led by withered rabbis who, in turn, bear little resemblance to the vibrant spirit of the early Hasidim who would rail at the edifice complex we Jews have today in constructing imposing synagogues and Jewish community centers. None of which is to say one era of Jews is superior or inferior to another. Only that there have been marked differences over the centuries and there is no reason this should not continue—*we Jews must evolve if we are to persist*.

The question becomes, how will this "new form" of Jewishness look? Jeffrey Rubin-Dorsky and Shelley Fisher Fishkin recently edited a collection of essays entitled, *People of the Book: Thirty Scholars Reflect on their Jewish Identity*. In it, they call for a "reconfiguration" of Judaism. But I submit this is not necessary.

What will provide the answer is a return to the essence of what made a person a Jew for the past thousands of years. This has been the unifying force of our People and it merely needs to be recognized like an old and dear friend. We have only but to look and this is what I set out to do here.

Why Be Jewish and How To Do It rests upon this foundation—established long before there were *halakhah* and festivals, temples and shuls—when Abraham, the great iconoclast, debunker, and radical monotheist, and later the prophets, following in his tradition, established precepts and provided a Jewish way of responding to life which emphasized a *oneness* and *unity* to the world. This is what it means to be a Jew and the responsibility it bears provides the reason to remain a Jew.

What is more, following the example of Bonnie Jacobs embracing Sheryl, we must look upon each other in an all-inclusive manner—leaving no one out. And while this means we must find common ground with the religious and observant Jew, it also means that there are millions of Jews like us for whom anything akin to organized religion is not palatable but for whom we do want our Jewishness to mean something. This has been expressed by Theo Richmond, author of *Konin*, where he writes: "I regret the absence of holiness in my own daily life, the spiritual vacuum, yet I cannot fill it with the divine, cannot pray. The result is a vague inner reaching for the transcendent that is perpetually frustrated."

Well, be frustrated no longer! In the pages to follow, I invite you, whether you be a Jew seeking to reinforce your Jewish identity or a Jew still in doubt if that identity should even be maintained or perhaps the non-Jewish spouse of a Jew wanting to become part of your mate's heritage or simply someone having an interest in Jewishness—please proceed as you would on an adventure where there is no set path to take and you make your own. And most of all, be assured everyone is warmly welcomed.

There is nothing judgmental here, for that is contrary to the Jewish nature of tolerance, freedom, and equality. You can be religious or not; belong to a synagogue or not; be an atheist or agnostic, a secularist, universalist, or humanist—or not. Feel free to choose from the cornucopia of adages, thoughts, and material in this book. It's for you to decide.

The first five Parts of this book—You Are Not Alone!; So Who Is A Jew Anyway?; Why Be A Jew? How About Our Values!; You Don't Have To Be Religious Or Believe In God To Be Jewish; and Something Missing? Try Jewish Spirituality—are designed to provide food for thought and address the question of why be a Jew in the first place. In addition to my own observations, you will find interspersed many sayings and maxims written by Jews of all ilk contemplating a myriad of subjects. Peruse it, read it, and reflect upon it. Keep in mind this is a starting point and we're all heading out together.

The last five Parts—How To Celebrate The Holidays And Why; Jewish Organizations—One Or More For You!; Reading And Being Jewish—Even On The Internet; Adult Education; and The Next Generation—Your Children—are meant to provide information and resources to enable you to maintain your Jewish identity in a way suited for you. This can be done by joining a Jewish group like B'nai B'rith or Hadassah. Or, you may prefer pursuing your Jewish identity by visiting Jewish web sites or reading books and periodicals of Jewish interest.

Our holidays have been with us for hundreds and even thousands of years and sometimes new meaning must be attached to them to make them important to you. Therefore, contemporary ways to celebrate the holidays are offered and suggestions made as to how you may go about doing this with particular emphasis upon doing so in your home. And naturally, given our proclivity toward the value of education—why not a Jewish education for you—the adult!

Even in the throes of questioning or struggling with your own Jewishness, it is very possible that you are still concerned about your children maintaining their Jewish identity and thus, the last part presents ways to help your children nurture a positive sense of being Jewish. Nonetheless, statistics have a way of coming back to haunt us and it is likely you will have to confront the question of intermarriage. This should be viewed as an opportunity to make a non-Jewish spouse feel welcome and join our community and share our heritage.

Why, just think, since there are more Jews intermarrying than are not, if we can turn things around and have a majority of children of such marriages raised Jewish, there will be an increase of Jews in later years. Now that, in and of itself, could do away with the threat of the "vanishing American Jew!"

Finally, the Appendix will provide a sample list of books of Jewish interest you may want to consider. After all, we are the "People of the Book!"

Now, let's embark on our journey as we Jews enter the fifth millennium of our existence as a People.

Part I

You Are Not Alone!

CHAPTER
1

Adrift in a Sea of Assimilation?

During the High Holidays, when a seemingly endless procession of Jews are parading to their synagogues accoutered in their finest apparel, are you overcome by a sense of isolation? Do you become convinced you're the only Jew in the world not davening to the heart-rending incantation of Kol Nidre?

What I generally do at such times is to put on a CD of Jewish music, set it at the track where Richard Tucker chants Kol Nidre, and ease back brimming with nostalgia. But it doesn't completely assuage the gnawing feeling inside me that I've become detached from the Jewish people—or at least a good many of them.

If the above or something similar to it describes what you have experienced, then I am here to tell you, feel that way no more! You are not alone. In the Introduction, I said that if you are unaffiliated with any Jewish organization or synagogue, you are one of more than half the Jews living in the United States. Then there are those Jews who are only nominal members of Jewish groups—say by writing a dues check once a year, or attending synagogue infrequently (the "three day a year Jew"). And what about those Jews who are affiliated but have doubts about the Jewish identity their affiliation provides? Add this together and you belong to a group comprising more than two thirds of this country's five and one half million Jews.

The problem is that despite the fact that there are upwards of three or four million of us, we're not very well organized. Sure, there are some organizations and groups of secular and humanistic Jews—and we'll get to this in Chapter 32—but for the most part, we are like millions of amoebae scurrying helter skelter, not aware the rest of us even exist.

I'm not advocating that we band together and create more Jewish associations and splinter the American Jewish community even further. But humans are by nature not solitary animals and some sense of kinship is part of what we seek. We must recognize that simply because we do not identify with a particular branch of Judaism such as "Conservative" or "modern Orthodox" or "Reform," does not mean we don't belong.

And just where is it exactly that we do belong? It's simple. You're a Jew. You are a member of the Jewish community. Just say it. "I am a Jew." Whether I declare it aloud to someone or breathe it to myself, I always feel good when I pronounce those words. What is more, you'll feel a part of something—belonging to a people who have identified themselves as such for four millennium.

Now, maybe you have had trouble speaking those words lately. Perhaps you don't even consider yourself a Jew at all anymore. Or, you still identify as a Jew but don't believe it to be a significant factor in what makes you who you are. There might even be negative connotations in the way you perceive being Jewish.

Because these are important concerns, before proclaiming, "I am a Jew," it is necessary we first examine these issues. If you are going to identify with those millions of Jews on the American landscape like yourself, you should do it with purpose and honesty for, as we shall see in Part Three, this is how we Jews operate.

So, let's explore what may be holding you back and hindering your ability to declare with pride and emotion, "I am a Jew."

CHAPTER
2

That "Old Time Religion"
Doesn't Work for You Anymore?

Diane was ahead of her time. Not that becoming a trailblazer was her idea but her parents wanted her to have a Hebrew school education and Diane, ever the dutiful daughter, did not object. Although this may not sound unusual today, conditions were different when Diane attended Hebrew school in the 1950s where she was one of only two girls in her class.

Diane grew accustomed to the smirks and taunts made by some of the jeering pre-adolescent boys. Yet, this did not prevent her from excelling in the course work. Although she had almost perfect attendance at the youth-run Sabbath services held in the basement chapel, Diane could not be called to the Torah nor have any of the other "honors" which were distributed among her classmates, let alone lead the service which she knew by heart.

Nonetheless, Diane was enraptured by the prayers and the history of her people. She loved the way the Hebrew words spilled from her tongue and she persevered, becoming one of the first girls ever to have a bat mitzvah in her synagogue. The event was held on a Friday night when the Torah remained in the ark so there would be no offense when Diane ascended to the pulpit. She arched her eyes from time to time to see her parents, bubbas, and zeydas *kvelling* in the front row. Diane loved the warm feeling being in synagogue always gave her and she went on to be confirmed three years later.

But after confirmation, things changed for Diane. Her inquisitiveness and thirst for knowledge absorbed everything offered in high school and college. She read books about religion, philosophy, and psychology and began to wonder about the prayers she had been saying every night before going to sleep when she asked God to watch over her loved ones. She questioned whether she believed in a deity—a male, no less—who considered the supplications offered from the world below. After a time, her answer was "no," and she would come to agree with Primo Levi where he wrote in *Survival In Auschwitz*, about a man he observed praying just after one of numerous "selections":

> *Silence slowly prevails and then . . . I see and hear old Kuhn praying aloud, with his beret on his head, swaying . . . violently. Kuhn is thanking God because he has not been chosen.*
>
> *Kuhn is out of his senses. Does he not see Beppo the Greek in the bunk next to him, Beppo is twenty years old and is going to the gas chamber the day after tomorrow and knows it. . . . Does Kuhn not understand that what has happened today is an abomination, which no propitiatory prayer, no pardon, no expiation by the guilty, which nothing at all in the powers of man can ever clean again?*
>
> *If I was God, I would spit at Kuhn's prayer.*

Despite her changed attitude toward prayer, Diane still attended synagogue with her parents on the holidays but the prayers chanted by the cantor and choir left her cold. By the time she married, she had no objection to skipping synagogue altogether on the holidays to be with her husband who, though Jewish, considered himself an agnostic.

Diane couldn't explain it but somehow, over the years, all that was religious had lost any meaning for her. When her first child approached the age to begin Hebrew school, she found herself in a predicament. Should she go along with most of her friends and join a synagogue—perhaps Reform—so her children could acquire the requisite Jewish education to qualify for the bar and bat mitzvahs? Or, perhaps she should seek alternatives. But where and what kind? Of course, there was always her husband's suggestion that they skip the entire archaic process altogether. What to do? Diane shook her head in a quandary.

Does Diane's dilemma sound familiar? Of course, your situation may be somewhat different. Or maybe a whole lot different! Possibly your experience in Hebrew school was not as enriching as Diane's. Perhaps it was just a place to misbehave and not worry about grades since it didn't count like regular school.

Yet, despite the fact you may look back at your Hebrew school years as boring and tedious, interfering with more pleasant after-school activities, there is something goading you to have your kids follow the tradition. How could they not have a bar or bat mitzvah? You ask yourself.

And, on those occasions where you find yourself in syna-gogue—perhaps as a guest at a bar mitzvah or on high holidays— you discover your lips still emit prayers embedded in your memory and you unconsciously hum the chants of your youth. Something alluring and familiar swells within your breast. You almost yearn to recapture a taste of that religious sensibility you once possessed but your mind tells you otherwise. Or, you follow the English translation and realize it would be hypocritical to take the prayers with any degree of seriousness. And yet . . . .

Then again, maybe you want nothing whatever to do with the religious rituals Judaism requires. You wash your hands of keeping kosher or observing the Sabbath or attending synagogue. You even eat bread on Passover! Judaism, or any religion, is simply not for you and therefore, you assume, neither is being Jewish.

But that's where you're wrong. You don't have to be religious or adhere to Judaism as a religion to be a Jew. This is something I will discuss at length in Part Four. On the other hand, there are many options and variations on the religious aspect of Judaism you may want to consider such as "Jewish spirituality" (Part Five), and nontra-ditional ways to celebrate the holidays (Part Six).

In any event, don't allow your rejection of Judaism or your disenchantment with religion to prevent you from maintaining and, if need be, resurrecting your Jewish identity. Take a lesson from the millions of secular Israeli Jews who are anything but religious. Although, theirs is an easier task not having to live in a country where ninety-eight out of every hundred people are not Jewish. We, on the other hand, must do more than say we're Jews to maintain our identity. Otherwise, we risk losing it.

Which is, of course, the predicament we're in. Just how do we go about maintaining our Jewish identity if the old time religion doesn't work for us anymore? Let's have a look. . . .

CHAPTER
3

Still Call Yourself a Jew
but Not Sure What to Do About It?

Hear the one about Irving Schwartz,who more than anything in the world loved to play golf? Unfortunately, the best course in the area belonged to one of the most prestigious country clubs which was essentially closed to Jews. Not to be deterred, Irving obtained a list of the club members hoping to discover a *landsman* or someone with a smattering of Jewish blood who might sponsor him. About a third of the way down, his heart raced as he blurted aloud the name, "David Green!"

His fingers barely able to dial the phone number, he reached David Green at his office. After introducing himself, he asked if Mr. Green would sponsor him for membership. "Why, you are a *landsman*, aren't you, Mr. Green?"

"Certainly not!" Blared the outraged voice.

"But . . . but your name's 'Green.' Shortened from 'Greenberg' or 'Greenbaum' or . . . or something like that, I thought . . . ." Schwartz stammered.

"Sir, I'm no kin of yours. And I'll have you know," the mortified voice intoned, "That my name has always been 'Green'; that 'Green' has always been my father's name; and, moreover, it had always been the name of my grandfather, *alav ha-sholom.*"

Unfortunately, we Jews have had our share of the likes of Mr. Green—quick to deny his Jewish heritage. Even worse, are those Jews whom we call "self-hating Jews" and often, arising from this self-hatred, they lash out at other Jews. History has been replete with numerous examples and, no doubt, you probably have come upon one or two yourself. And while you don't necessarily go around waving the Israeli flag or introducing yourself as being a Jew, you deplore those Jews who are full of loathing or shame for anything Jewish.

In fact, there are even times when you, often unconsciously, proclaim your Jewishness to the world. Maybe it's the Star of David or Chai you wear around your neck, especially when strolling along the beach where it's there for everyone to see. Or perhaps, in a conversation, although you don't speak Yiddish, you let a Yiddishism slip in here or there, like an *oy veh* or *gevalt* and you smack your forehead. And what about adding a *kineahorah* when uttering a fortuitous announcement, even though you're unsure of its exact translation and you're not superstitious.

Yet, unlike our "Mr. Green," while you still call yourself a Jew, you are at a loss regarding what to do about your Jewish identity. In fact, your Jewishness has become no more than a piece of wardrobe you wear from time to time depending on the occasion and the circumstances. Deep down inside, you sense this doesn't fit right and this bothers you.

You want to be a Jew but know there is something unfulfilling when being Jewish consists only of affixing a mezuzah to the right front door jam of your home or employing a Yiddish word or phrase or perfunctorily going through the drill an annual visit to the synagogue demands. You want more. You want being Jewish to mean something beyond that.

Even more, you squirm under the defiant stares emanating from your children who are no longer accepting, just on your say-so, that they remain Jewish like you. Which, of course, is part of the problem. That being "like you," since you're not quite sure yourself what it means to be Jewish. And that being the case, how can you possibly convey Jewishness to them?

Bottom line is there must be more to being a Jew than what you've got. At least, so you hope. The good news is, *there is* more to being Jewish than going through the motions. This I promise and we'll get to it just as soon as we dispel one or two other notions holding some of you back from proudly proclaiming and living your Jewish identity.

CHAPTER
4

So You're No Longer a Jew but a Member of the Greater Human Community and Yet . . .

In the best of worlds, we would be equally concerned about every human life regardless of nationality, race, or religion. Implicit in this position is the concept that we are all part of the greater human community and the schisms we have created have done more harm than good. Certainly, there is much to be said for breaking down the barriers which divide people and occasionally give rise to conflict—even deadly conflict.

For many of us this argument makes sense and for some, as a result, you have discarded your Jewishness like an old and frayed raincoat. It served its purpose and kept you dry from the rain. But now the sun is out and not a shower in sight so who needs it any longer?

Time for a reality check. Although I do not advocate maintaining your Jewish identity solely in response to anti-semitism (Chapter 6), given what history has demonstrated and absent a total transformation in human nature, divisions among the humans populating this planet are likely to remain a permanent fixture for the foreseeable future.

While a grand scheme of uniformity in the world may at first blush appear as a desirable goal, frankly, I'm not so sure. Which would you prefer to wear? A somber gray coat or a coat of varied hues—bright and bold and beautiful? The bleak coat of an undertaker or Joseph's wondrous coat of many colors?

This has been put another way by Mordecai Kaplan, whose writings in the mid-twentieth century gave rise to the Reconstructionist movement. Kaplan believed every religion and civilization has a unique contribution to make to the greater human community which results in certain values held by all. Rather than try to make ourselves indistinguishable from one another, we ought to celebrate and respect our differences.

Further, Kaplan maintains, Jews have managed to exist for thousands of years, often under extreme adversity, because we have given a universal significance to our own values (Chapter 9). So while a belief in universal values is nothing new to being Jewish, it does not follow that we renounce our own particular heritage in favor of the phantasm of a oneness/sameness of humanity.

This has been echoed by Primo Levi in a conversation he had with Philip Roth in 1986, a year before Levi's death:

> *Italian Jews (but the same can be said of the Jews of many other nations) made an important contribution to their country's cultural and political life without renouncing their identity, in fact by keeping faith with their cultural tradition. To possess two traditions, as happens to Jews but not only to Jews, is a richness . . . .*

And by the way, have you ever noticed what often happens to those of us Jews who express these universal goals and eschew ethnocentricity? Somewhere along the line, generally with advancing years, there is at least a slight acknowledgment of those Jewish roots. Perhaps it has to do with a growing wisdom which comes with age, or a disillusionment with world events, or an increasing sense of mortality which prompts one to return to one's traditions.

Another possibility is something I call the "Jewish soul" which may lie somewhere within your genes or DNA and is a part of you. I'll discuss this in Chapter 8. In any event, once in a while, this Jewish thing kicks in and nudges you to acknowledge your Jewishness despite the fact you are a citizen of the world.

If you are a person who believes in the universality of humanity, allow me to assure you this is no reason to prevent you from maintaining and even nurturing your Jewish identity. Believe me, you can still pursue the ideals of a united human race and remain a Jew, which we will discover in the pages to follow.

But first, there's one piece of unfinished business to address. This has to do with a specific segment of the Jewish community. In fact, I must confess to belonging to this group, for it is with the "Baby Boomers" that the decline in our Jewish population truly began.

CHAPTER
5

Blame It on Us Baby Boomers!

If you belong to the generation born in the years following World War II, the turbulent events which took place from the mid-sixties through the mid-seventies may well have had a great impact upon you. During those years, a conflagration spread from coast to coast in this land: flags were set ablaze; bras were burned; draft cards went up in smoke. Police were "pigs;" politicians were "murderers" commissioning an ignominious war; complying with the Protestant Ethic meant "selling out;" authority, once accepted unquestionably whether exercised by police, teachers, or parents, was blatantly defied; and more pertinent to the topic at hand, religion became, as Marx phrased it, the "opium of the masses" while the cover of *Time Magazine* blazoned Nietzche's phrase, "God is Dead."

In other words, "God, mother, and apple pie" was replaced with "Sartre, free love, and pot." And for no group was this more applicable than the Jews. Perhaps this is so because we are a people with an iconoclastic disposition, forever questioning what others accept on blind faith (Chapter 10). Far out of proportion to the general population, these young Jews thumbed their noses at sheriffs and their deputies in Selma, Alabama; taunted and spit at Mayor Daley's club-wielding police in Chicago; and while engaged in a surreal effort to levitate the Pentagon, stuffed daisies down the rifle barrels of U.S. Army troops.

Existentialism pervaded many of this generation of Jews. What mattered was the here and now and doing something about it. Religion became obsolete. Praying to God was a "cop out" when what was needed was action. And despite the activism of those like Rabbi Abraham Joshua Heschel, the Jewish religious establishment was far removed from the loop of the civil disobedience called for in those tumultuous times.

Hence, for generally the noblest of motives, religion and Jewish identity was tossed aside. If not viewed with outright disdain like all other religions, Judaism was simply not a factor in pursuing the meritorious goals of peace and equality, despite the fact that these are so integral to Jewish values (Part Three).

No doubt, this contempt for the status quo, which encompassed religion and ethnicity in the minds of many baby boomers, contributed to the decline of the Jewish population. The intermarriage rate soared for this generation and, as we have seen, the children of these marriages were generally not raised Jewish. And even where both parents were Jewish, their children were frequently provided a tenuous Jewish identity at best.

But we're older now, though not necessarily wiser. As the first of us have begun to cross the half century mark, we peer more frequently at the past, our forebearers, and our heritage while, with the other eye, we gaze upon our children, who are beginning to marry and have families of their own.

Despite all the slogans and clichés of those times gone by and how they became part of what we hold true and dear, more and more of us are saddened when witnessing our children and grandchildren look upon their Jewish heritage with no more than a glance. Moreover, we experience a sense of loss with the growing prospect that Jews may all but vanish from this country.

We may not always be able to articulate why, but this is how we feel and we want to do something about it. But given our tradition, we must have reasons before taking action. Simply trying to cram Jewishness down the throats of the next generation would be hypocritical and contrary to our values. This is what Part Three is designed to address.

However, before we arrive at that destination, there is one rather important matter to be clarified. When we speak of Jews disappearing from this nation, just whom are we speaking about? And when you look into the mirror and ask whether or not you are still a Jew, what do you mean by a "Jew?"

So, before moving on, let us ponder and perhaps even answer the interminable question which has seemed to confound and baffle even the wisest of rabbis, theologians, and philosophers, in fact, just about everybody—"Who is a Jew?"

Part II

So Who Is a Jew Anyway?

CHAPTER
6

Don't Be Jewish out of Spite

In a piece he wrote for the *Forward*, Joseph Epstein referred to Sartre's reactive definition that a Jew is "anyone whom other people thought of as a Jew." Epstein went on to say that he is such a Jew but with "a positive spin" and identifiable by "outlook and style of thought."

It is easy to be a Jew out of spite responding to anti-semitism. Which is why for most of our history, Jews have never had an identity problem. The world has had a knack for singling us out—usually in negative ways, whether depicting us in sketches with hooked beaks for noses, horns on our heads, and cloven hoofs for feet, or isolating us in ghettos and pummeling us with pogroms. Sometimes the means were more subtle, like excluding us from their country clubs, business enterprises, colleges, and professional schools.

Clearly, the Holocaust brought this to epic proportions. As Tovah Reich has her fanatical Jewish character proclaim in her novel, *The Jewish War*: "The Holocaust taught . . . that every single Jew without exception was hunted down."

But in the United States today, where by and large Jews are accepted as part of the American community, it won't do to hang our Jewish identity on the negative. There has to be something more. Consider the following:

Because of the assimilated life of my entire family, all I knew about being a Jew was that I and all of my closest friends . . . had to suffer from the taunts, the rejection and occasionally the open aggression of some of our gentile schoolmates and even some of our teachers. Now, suddenly [after reading Martin Buber], my Jewishness has a positive content.

—Bruno Bettelheim

But what is my belief? Why don't I know? Maybe because my life has been too easy, and men in robes have never forced me back on my faith. But I should not need a torture chamber to know what I believe.

—Daniel Evan Weiss

Unlike the entrenched anti-semitism faced by Bruno Bettelheim in early twentieth century Austria, and more in keeping with the milieu of the contemporary American novelist, Daniel Evan Weiss, most Jews in this country born after 1960 have never experienced anti-semitism or, if so, it has been relatively mild and insidious. To the extent this has removed the "Jewish" crown of thorns foisted upon us by most countries and cultures over the centuries, this has been beneficial. But we are also presented with a challenge. For instead of being a Jew in reaction to others, as Sartre observed, now we must arrive at our own destination in determining who we are.

Hence, we reach the question, "Who is a Jew?" Let's have a look.

CHAPTER
7

Here's What Others Have to Say About "Who Is a Jew?"

My sons attended a Jewish folkshul where they learned Jewish history, traditions, and values but there was no prayer, no Torah, no synagogue. For their bar mitzvahs, they each selected a subject, were tutored for a year, and then made a presentation to friends, family, and the entire shula community. My older son, Cory, decided upon the topic, "Who Is a Jew?"

He addressed all the possibilities such as the requirement of being born of a Jewish mother; having a belief in one God; adherence to the Ten Commandments; or following *halakhah*. Cory's conclusion, reached at the age of thirteen and which has been repeated by more renown and erudite figures although in sophistic terms, was this: "If you are born a Jew, that is, of at least one Jewish parent; believe strongly that you are a Jew; and you choose to remain a Jew—then you are a Jew."

When I approach a conundrum, I like to think of simple solutions. It seems to me that if nothing else, all Jews can and do agree on one thing—Abraham (or at least his legendary figure) was the first Jew. Given this, we can follow a rather straightforward line of inquiry.

If Abraham was the first Jew, this would mean his parents were not Jewish. Therefore, the necessity of being born of a Jewish mother must fail. Moreover, Abraham did not follow the ten commandments nor observe *halakhah* since there were no such concepts at that time. Nor were the Torah, Talmud, and Mishna even glints in God's eye. Abraham did not keep kosher nor eat only unleavened bread on Passover nor fast on Yom Kippur. Why, there weren't any Jewish holidays to observe at all—not even the Sabbath!

So what made Abraham a Jew? It's just as the Bible tells us—he broke, decimated, and otherwise smashed idols to bits. He refused to believe that these statues were divine. In other words, Abraham was an iconoclast. There was nothing to which he owed blind obedience or absolute devotion. Everything was open to question.

But Abraham did believe in one God. The problem was he knew nothing more about this God—not even His/Her name. All he knew was this was the one and only God. Abraham was a radical monotheist.

What worked for Abraham is good enough for me. I consider myself to be an iconoclast and radical monotheist knowing absolutely nothing about God other than God's oneness. Everything else is dicta.

Which is not to say this is the best answer and certainly no better than Cory's. After all, while this issue has been hotly debated over the centuries—now more than ever, no clear-cut resolution has emerged to gain substantial acceptance.

Others have equally worthwhile insights on this question. I offer you the opinions of a number of Jews as food for thought. Mull them over and reach your own conclusions or better yet, bring them up for discussion with friends and family and see what develops.

Many believe that what makes us Jews, who we are, has to do with having been cast in the role of the outsider for so long. The result is that we Jews are dubious of authority and ready to question rather than "merely follow orders." The Jew is, for the most part, anything but a "true believer."

We come by this naturally, for such is our tradition beginning with Abraham and exemplified in twentieth century America with the inordinate number of Jews who filled the ranks of the trade unionist movement or were hauled before McCarthy's HUAC hearings or marched for civil rights in the South or protested the Vietnam War.

There is, after all, a reason we are called the "stiff-necked" people and we will discuss this further in Chapter 10 when we consider Jewish values. But for now, consider the following:

> Jewish identity signifies a sense of common ancestry, of kinship, of shared memories, of shared danger and vulnerability. The other tradition was skeptical and even angry and distrustful of authority. One of the legacies . . . is Yiddish humor which is irreverent.
>
> —Max Rosenfeld

> To me, the Jew and his questioning are one. He devises systems and immediately questions their validity; he refuses to be categorized. To be a Jew, therefore, is to ask a question—a thousand questions, yet always the same—of society, of others, of oneself, of death and of God.
>
> —Elie Wiesel

> If Yahweh would have wanted me to be calm, he would have made me a goy.
>
> —Philip Roth

Over the centuries since our inception as a people, there have been certain values Jews have held and, while these will be discussed in Part Three, these attributes have come to be a part of who we are. They lend themselves in defining our own identity.

> The bond that has united the Jews for thousands of years and that unites them today is, above all, the democratic ideal of social justice, coupled with the ideal of mutual aid and tolerance among all. . . . The second characteristic trait of Jewish tradition is the high regard in which it holds every form of intellectual aspiration and spiritual effort.
>
> —Albert Einstein

> The preference which through two thousand years the Jews have given to spiritual endeavor has, of course, had its effect; it has helped to build a dike against brutality and the inclination to violence.
>
> —Sigmund Freud

Jewishness in my family meant reverence for books and intelligence. It meant the superiority of knowledge to ignorance, kindness to brutality. It meant you had sympathy for anyone who suffered because Jews suffered and that you fought against bigotry.
                                        —*Alicia Ostriker*

The Jews gave to the world its three greatest religions, reverence for law, and the highest conceptions of morality. Our teaching of brotherhood and righteousness has, under the name of democracy and social justice, become the twentieth century ideal of America and Western Europe.
                                        —*Louis D. Brandeis*

The Jews had chosen themselves . . . to lead sanctified lives, without wars, without adultery, without mockery or rebellion. But could their behavior serve as an example for others? Yes. . . . Humanity could abolish warfare, divide the land so that there would be enough for everyone. Each group could have its language, its culture, its traditions. But one thing all would have to have in common: a belief in one God and in free will; a discipline that would transform all men's deeds into serving God and helping one another.
                                        —*Isaac Bashevis Singer*

We are a people who stand for a certain thing, a certain sense of justice and freedom. . . . We must do right by the world. We must not treat the world as the world treats us.
                                        —*Richard Dreyfuss*

Jews and Jewishness add a palpably positive dimension to the places they inhabit. Our collective experiences, especially with persecution, have made many Jews especially sensitive to the suffering of others, to the need for equality for all, to the virtues of compassion toward those less fortunate, to the appreciation of creativity and education. . . .
                                        —*Alan Dershowitz*

In the end, when it comes right down to it, perhaps the most identifying feature about being a Jew is something that cannot be defined or easily put into words. It is a feeling—a sense of community and belonging to a family. We started out as a tribe of nomads with Abraham at the lead and we followed his footsteps even when he wasn't sure where he was going. This didn't matter because we were together and forged a common affinity for each other which would serve to hold us in place for the thousands of years we would wander the face of the Earth during the Diaspora. All that is really necessary about being a Jew is acknowledging this and recognizing a kinship with fellow Jews.

An evil that has always afflicted my people's history . . . internal Jewish schism . . . Pharisees against the Sadducees, Maskilim against the Hasidim, Bundists against Zionists. What about the Jewish solidarity so praised in our literature?

Yet I believed in it. In my eyes, to be a Jew was to belong to the Jewish community in the broadest sense and most immediate sense. It was to feel abused whenever a Jew . . . was humiliated. It was to react, to protest, whenever a Jew, even an unknown Jew in some distant land, was attacked for the simple reason that he was a Jew.

—*Elie Wiesel*

A Jew is someone who regards himself as a Jew, or someone who is forced to be a Jew. If he does not acknowledge any connection with the Jewish people . . . he is not a Jew . . . even if religious law defines him as such because his mother is Jewish. A Jew, in my unhalakhic opinion, is someone who chooses to share the fate of other Jews, or who is condemned to do so. And finally, to be a Jew means to feel that whenever a Jew is persecuted for being a Jew—that means you.

—*Amos Oz*

Shall we call a man Jewish who lived and worked among the gentiles and sold them pig meat . . . and not once in twenty years comes inside a synagogue? I will say, 'Yes—Morris Bober was to me a true Jew because he lived in the Jewish experience, which he remembered, and with the Jewish heart.' Maybe not to our formal tradition—for this I don't excuse him—but he was true to the spirit of our life—to want for others that which he wants also for himself.

—*Bernard Malamud*

Israel is a community, a people, not a collection of individual selves. The conviction that personhood is shaped, nourished, and sustained in community is a central assumption that Judaism and feminism share.

                                       —*Judith Plaskow*

So, who is a Jew? What are the essential ingredients? I leave it to you to decide for yourself. As for whether or not you are a Jew, so far as I am concerned, if you say you are a Jew and are taking the trouble to be reading this book, it's enough for me.

Whatever it is that makes us the Jews we are, it has proven to be enduring, at least thus far in our history. And perhaps, as Elie Wiesel suggests, this is also a part of what it means to be a Jew:

Who is a Jew? A Jew is he — or she — whose song cannot be muted, whose joy cannot be killed by the enemy . . . ever.

CHAPTER
8

Phylogeny, Genes,
and the Jewish Soul

History is replete with Jews who have shed their Jewishness. While some have done so by outright conversion, most have simply ceased considering themselves Jews; like Josef Kalyika, a character in Kevin Baker's novel *Dreamland*, who declared: "I don't want to be a Jew anymore. I'm through with it."

Easier said then done, Josef, as thousands of assimilated European Jews discovered at the hands of the Nazis even though their only Jewish ancestry was one grandparent. But it's more than a matter of how others view us. Rather, it is something within—something you are born with which cannot be summarily discarded like an old coat or worn hat.

Intuitively, the early Hebrews knew this—that some things were passed on from one generation to the next with the simple and natural act of procreating. One of these things, they believed, had to do with whatever it is that makes a person a Jew.

Thus, until recently, Jewish identity was a simple matter. For a time, it meant that if you were born of a Jewish father, you were Jewish. Wait, did I say "father?" Yes, I did, and this shouldn't surprise you. After all, if Jewishness was derived from the mother, than Moses' progeny would not be Jewish because his wife, Zipporah, was a Midianite.

Jewish law today however, and for most of our history, places Jewish identity upon matriarchal lineage. As to why this is so, I leave to the rabbis. But it seems to me one good reason is because there can never be a doubt as to who is one's mother. While on the other hand, as for the natural father, suffice it to say, things may not always be as they appear.

But this is beside the point. The thing is, there has always been this belief in the bloodline and just as physical features are passed on, so are other attributes and dispositions.

Although there is something almost mystical about this belief, it is not without reasoned and scientific explanations as well. In the early nineteenth century, the respected French naturalist, Jean Lamarck, put forth his theory of acquired characteristics or phylogeny, in which he held new traits developed by an organism are transmitted to their offspring. Although this was later largely rejected by the scientific community, Freud based much of his theory upon this Lamarckian proposition to the extent he held that within an individual psyche lies an archaic residue of the entire human race. In recent times, we have spoken more in terms of genes and heredity and currently, we talk about DNA, which carries all that makes up an individual human being.

While this is far afield from my area of expertise, it doesn't take a rocket scientist to conclude that all evidence has been pointing to the fact that much of who we are is inherited. And without getting into the "environment vs. heredity" debate, I think it safe to conclude that at least some basic features are passed on from one generation to the next though they may be tempered and altered by one's milieu.

Consider how the Yiddish writer, Miriam Raskin, described a character in one of her short stories: "She had a *yiddishe neshoma*, a Jewish soul. . . . What else would you call her concern for 'higher matters' or her readiness to make sacrifices for the things she believed in? There was always an air of exalted spirituality about her, as if she bore a heavy responsibility for the world."

Whether or not there is a "soul," let alone a "Jewish soul," is something I leave to you and Chapter 21. But I do believe that whatever it is that has made Jews be Jews—emotionally, cognitively, and culturally—is something you are born with at least to some extent.

And as the character in A.B. Yehoshua's novel, *Mr. Mani*, discovered after he proclaimed, "I was Jewish, but I am not anymore . . . I've canceled it. . . ." Being Jewish is something one just doesn't "cancel."

Part III

Why Be a Jew?
How About Our Values!

CHAPTER
9

We Are "One"

Sh'ma Yisrael Adonai Eloheynu Adonai Echad.
Hear O Israel, the Lord our God, the Lord is One.

The *Sh'ma* is prayed at every synagogue service. Over the centuries, it has been proclaimed by Jews as their last profession of faith before being burned at the stakes by crusaders, or flayed by Cossacks, or shot by Nazis at the edge of gaping pits. It is presumed to be the central tenet of all Jews, religious or not, and in fact, it is just that.

While the *Sh'ma* has been and continues to be expressed and thought of in diverse ways, by its very nature, it is just one thing—a statement of universality searing through time and space serving as a continual reminder that all pieces are part of the whole. Or, in the words of the nineteenth century Hasidic master, Rabbi Nachman of Bratslav: "All things have one root."

Clearly, the *Sh'ma* is a declaration of monotheism and it is this belief in One God that is the foremost Jewish contribution to the human race. In Chapter 16, we will consider in greater detail whether you have to believe in God to be Jewish but suffice it to say here that this affirmation in One God must be read liberally. For example, consider the following:

The Sh'ma *is not addressed to God. It is a call to Israel, to our-selves, and to those around us. This is the highest unity, the inner gate of oneness. According to the* Sh'ma, *all is One. . . . Nothing but the One exists.*

—Rabbi Arthur Green

Things are all connected with one another. . . . There is nothing but God and His works. . . . There is no way of knowing God but through His works, and these prove His Being or existence.

—Maimonides

All things, which are, are in God, and nothing can either be or conceived without God.

—Spinoza

The oneness of creation, to my sense, is God.

—Albert Einstein

We will examine Jewish mysticism and spirituality in Part Five but you should be aware that this aspect of our heritage is based upon the Jewish emphasis on the "Oneness" of all Life. In explaining the Kabbalah, Jewish mysticism, Arthur Waskow put it this way:

Divine energy poured into the void, creating an utterly harmonious seamless vessel of supernal light—a holy universe. But God-energy was so intense that its very holiness shattered the vessel it was shaping. The seamless vessel of supernal light exploded into infinite sparks.

At the root of every soul, every act, every relationship in the universe we live in . . . is the darkened spark of holiness in exile. It is, said the kabbalists, our human task—though with God's help—to gather the sparks, to bring them back into the holy whole. . . .

You may perceive this notion of holy light and an infinite number of dispersed sparks either literally or metaphorically. Either way, the point is, we Jews have this basic way of looking at the world with everything being connected somehow. Or, perhaps, as uncon-nected, but with our help, destined to be restored.

Sometimes, in lieu of sparks of holy light, the metaphor is the human body:

The world of humanity is meant to become a single body; but it is as yet nothing more than a heap of limbs each of which is of the opinion that it constitutes the entire body. We are charged to perfect our own portion of the universe—the human world.

—Martin Buber

As Man's body consists of members and parts of various ranks all acting and reacting upon each other so as to form one organism, so does the world at large consist of a hierarchy of created things, which when they properly act and react upon each other together form literally one organic body.

—The Zohar

This Jewish emphasis on "Oneness" is not limited to the mystical nor something to be read metaphorically. It has very concrete applications regarding the way we relate to others, both human and nonhuman; how we conduct ourselves and develop our code of ethics and morality; how we go about getting through difficult times. This has been expressed in the twentieth century in a variety of ways. Perhaps one or more of the following will speak to you and cause you to appreciate this preeminent Jewish value.

What we need is not only the belief in one God but also the awareness of the one mankind, the awareness of the unity of humanity. I would call it "mon-anthropism."

—Viktor Frankl

This mystical feeling of the interdependence of human souls was forged in the gloomy prison-camp when our solidarity was the one weapon we had to oppose the world of evil. I formulated for myself a new law: the law of universal attraction, interconnection, and interdependence of human souls.

—Natan Sharansky

I regard nation states as a bad system. We ought to be building a polyphonic world. . . . Our human condition should at long last

evoke a sense of human solidarity. . . . Flag patriotism must give
way to humanity.

                                                      —Amos Oz

It is the Jewish emphasis on the sense of "Oneness" which has
led many people, Jews and Gentiles, to reach the conclusion that this
unity encompasses all living creatures thus giving rise to vegetarianism. Two of the great writers of this century (both Jews and
vegetarians), have phrased it this way:

> *We must aspire to the sort of internationalism which is founded*
> *upon a knowledge of other people and understanding of their*
> *essential differences and a religious love of all creatures. One will*
> *never rise to true spirituality if one looks down on any of God's*
> *creatures, if one considers them merely meat to devour and quar-*
> *ries to be hunted.*
>   *Vegetarianism is a major step on the road to peace. There*
> *is only one little step from killing animals to erecting gas*
> *chambers. . . . There will be no justice as long as man will stand*
> *with a knife or with a gun and destroy those who are weaker than*
> *he is.*
>
>   *—Isaac Bashevis Singer*

> *Now at last I can look at you in peace. I don't eat you anymore.*
>   *—Franz Kafka (to a fish)*

From our patriarch Abraham, who debunked all idols and false
gods for the One God, to us Jews living at the beginning of a new
millennium four thousand years later, the prominence placed upon
the concept of "Oneness" by our people has never diminished,
though it sometimes has assumed different forms. In the language
used to express so much that is Jewish, a Yiddish proverb states it in
utter simplicity:

> *Mir zenen geknipt un gebinden . . .*
> *We are knotted and bound to one another.*

CHAPTER
10

No Golden Calves for Us!

Jews have sometimes been derided for being a "stiff-necked" people—stubborn and headstrong. As if this were an intrinsic flaw in our collective character. But I look at it differently. The way I see it, we Jews hold a tenacious belief in the importance of the individual and possess an aversion to servility. That is why our necks are stiff. We don't bend and grovel to those who demand our absolute allegiance.

And I suppose the first "stiff neck" among us Jews stretches back to Abraham, who set a mighty fine example personifying Jewish values. Although he is best known for encountering YHWH, the One God, and entering into a covenant with Him/Her, there was a critical first step enabling our patriarch to reach that point.

First and foremost, Abraham was an iconoclast. He shattered the hand-made idols of the false gods by using common sense and not being afraid of raising a ruckus. Nor was he concerned about what others might think of him or that he might be ostracized from his community. For Abraham, the search for truth was uppermost in his mind and this provided the courage to confront the status quo.

Centuries later, when the Hebrews made their exodus from Egypt and stood at the foot of Mt. Sinai, a healthy skepticism was imbedded into the Jewish soul which reinforced our spirit of iconoclasm. This took the form of the Second Commandment:

Thou shalt have no other gods before Me. Thou shalt not make unto thee a graven Image . . . thou shalt not bow down unto them, nor serve them. . . .

It doesn't matter whether you believe the Decalogue was the word of God or drafted by Moses or written by one or more Hebrews centuries later. The important point is that we Jews have chosen to make this injunction a chief component in our value system. What is more, we have expanded it to go beyond golden calves depicting other deities.

In other words, "gods" and "graven image" are meant to be anything to which we are asked to give blind loyalty. This encompasses systems of belief, countries, generals barking commands, politicians enacting unjust laws, and so on. It can also be worshipping money and material objects, making gods out of the accumulation of wealth and possessions.

For a Jew to say he or she was "only following orders" would be to fly in the face of everything Jewish. That six million Jews were victims of murderers using this as an excuse for their crimes is no small irony for who but the Jew is the natural enemy of unconditional obedience. To take to task one's government or country or elected leaders regarding what one considers immoral actions has always been one of our most precious Jewish values.

Even God is open to question. When Woody Allen says, "To you I'm an atheist. To God I'm the loyal opposition," he is acting within Jewish tradition. By acknowledging God as a worthy adversary, Allen is conceding the possibility of His/Her existence and when daring to question God, he stands in the shadow of Job.

The list of Jews who have challenged the prevalent attitudes and precepts of their times is almost endless. Mordecai risked death refusing to bow and swear fealty to Haman. Spinoza set his sights upon the world with everything open to question and was excommunicated for daring to do so. Freud offended the scientific community, the proper Viennese society in which he lived, and even the Jewish establishment with his unrelenting questioning of things held sacrosanct. More recently and closer to home, Betty Friedan galvanized women across this nation to challenge the roles to which they had been consigned since the beginning of "his" story.

During the last four millennia, Jews have consistently played the part of the world's debunkers with nothing beyond the scope of our inquiring minds. This has been poignantly recognized by Germany's greatest lyric poet, Heinrich Heine; although he converted to Protestantism hoping to make a living as a university professor, he never considered himself a Christian, as the following, written near the end of his life, suggests:

> The writer of these pages [can] be proud that his ancestors belong to the noble house of Israel, that he is a descendant of martyrs, who gave the world a God and a moral code and who fought and suffered on all the battlefields of thought.

Heine was correct in accentuating the risk inherent in the role Jews assumed as they challenged established norms and canons. Sometimes, this resulted in Jews being declared enemies of the state and/or religious establishment, shunting them to the periphery of society, or subjecting them to inquisitions, pogroms, and even sentences of death.

We Jews have this way of occasionally making others feel uncomfortable, if not downright hostile. Because we dare to ask the difficult questions. Because we do not adhere to false idols. This has been expressed by two twentieth century Jewish writers who, in other respects, have little in common:

> The aim of the literature I call testimony is to disturb. I disturb the believer because I dare to put questions to God, the source of all faith. I disturb the miscreant because, despite my doubts and questions, I refuse to break with the religious and mystical universe that has shaped my own. Most of all, I disturb those who are comfortably settled within a system—be it political, psychological, or theological. If I have learned anything in my life, it is to distrust intellectual comfort.
>
> —Elie Wiesel

> He'd never lost the simple pleasure, which went way back, of making people uncomfortable, comfortable people especially.
>
> —Philip Roth

Being a Jew and an iconoclast go hand in hand. Through the centuries, Jews have demonstrated this—often paying a heavy price. Not long ago, this occurred with great drama and forcefulness when an entire nation was awakened from its slumber to end an unjust war. Jews, who for the most part were anything but religious, were at the forefront of the protests against this nation's actions in Vietnam.

Two such Jews, rather brazen individuals who were deeply involved in the antiwar movement, have stated the matter succinctly:

Irreverence is our only sacred cow.

                                  —Paul Krassner

Sacred cows make the tastiest hamburger.

                                  —Abbie Hoffman

We Jews have no golden calves. Nor, for that matter, do we have sacred cows. It goes against our nature and the essence of what it means to be a Jew.

CHAPTER
11

We Jews Revere Memory

Ever wonder why Jews have the habit of naming their children after deceased relatives and not, as the Gentiles do, in honor of someone living? Could be that it's a morbid infatuation with the dead but it is really something quite different. This practice has to do with the recognition Jews have regarding the connection we, who are alive today, share with our ancestors, with those just born, and with those yet to be.

This has been expressed quite well by the great Yiddish writer, Yitzhak Leib Peretz:

> *A people without a memory is like an individual with amnesia. An individual is a ringlet in the net which is spread over a certain spot on earth. The net is an individual's generation. And a person's generation is just a ringlet in the chain of generations which reaches back to . . . Abraham and extends onwards to the end of time.*

It is human nature to forget—especially that which is unpleasant. In fact, it was a Jew, Sigmund Freud, whose concept of repression exposed this defense mechanism. Although Freud and psychoanalysis has come under some criticism of late, the principle of repression remains one of the cornerstones of modern psychology and a key to comprehending what makes humans tick.

So, why do Jews have this tendency to remember—especially when our history is fraught with so much that renders anguish to the heart and torment to the soul? What's so wonderful about a history of persecution, torture, and genocide? Other peoples tend to recount how great their ancestors were; how powerful they were; how much wealth they possessed. What have we to brag about? Shtetls? Dispersion from our homeland lasting for almost two millennia? Sojourners in the lands of others subject to their whims? Were we awesome and mighty?

No. We were vagabonds meandering the face of the Earth. Tolerated at best; persecuted as a norm; murdered at worst. And yet, we recognize the need to remember. We have repeated for thousands of years how we were once slaves in Egypt. We recount how we were at the mercy of the crusaders who delighted in splitting open the bellies of pregnant Jewish women or burning the men at the stakes. We dwell on the pogroms pitting bloodthirsty Cossacks against terrified bearded Jews. And then came the Shoah—the slaughter of six million of us by methodically minded Nazis and their accomplices.

What makes us surmount this natural human inclination of suppressing such distress? Why go to the other extreme—practically flaunting these memories before the world and teaching them to our children so they'll never forget?

Why do we remember? Consider this:

The Ba'al Shem Tov . . . once said: "Forgetting is exile. . . ." In the light of twentieth century history, I would amend that axiom: Forgetting is not exile; forgetting is the Final Solution.

—Theo Richmond

It is human nature to forget what hurts you. . . . Without it, life would be intolerable. . . . But the Jews live by other rules. For a Jew, nothing is more important than memory. He is bound to his origins by memory. It is memory that connects him to Abraham, Moses and Rabbi Akiba. If he denies memory he will have denied his honor.

—Elie Wiesel

But it is not only honor we would be disavowing. In forgetting, especially the killing of our ancestors for the sole reason they were Jews, we would be deprecating their very existence. We would be desecrating their lives—denying that they had lived at all. And this, I suggest, goes against everything for which a Jew stands. For what else is important if not a life—any life—let alone one to whom we are linked.

To forget is to reject. To remember is to affirm. We, as Jews, recognize this and thus each time we recall the lives and events and history of our people, we validate their very existence—we imbue their lives with meaning. And in doing so and by passing on this value to the next generation, perhaps one day in the future, some Jew will recollect our existence and in so doing, confirm us.

CHAPTER
12

Peace, Harmony, and Understanding
It's the Jewish Way

The prophet Micah beheld a wondrous vision for when we reach the end of days:

> *They shall beat their swords into plowshares, and their spears into pruning-hooks; nation shall not lift up sword against nation, neither shall they learn war any more.*

Although peace is esteemed by all religions and peoples, more wars and acts of violence have been conducted in the name of religion than anything else (witness the Crusades, jihads, Muslim versus Hindu in Pakistan/India, Protestant versus Catholic in Ireland, and so on). Nor is Jewish history free from warfare. Indeed, the Old Testament contains just about the bloodiest narratives of battles and combat as one is likely to encounter in any tome.

Nonetheless, peace and harmony among all people is something Jews have proclaimed and striven for with great passion. What is more, Jews have a rather exalted notion of what peace involves and some unique means of arriving there. As Martin Buber put it:

A peace that comes about through cessation of war is no real peace. A great peace means cooperation. . . . People must engage in talk with one another . . . if the great peace is to appear.

The idea that respect for others and their differences forms the foundation for true peace has been articulated in a slightly different fashion by Louis D. Brandeis:

No peace which is lasting can ever come until the nations, great and small, accept . . . the truth that each people has in it something of peculiar value which it can contribute to that civilization for which we are all striving.

This grand conception of peace we Jews hold is accomplished by going beyond respecting others. It entails an emphasis on interpersonal relations and the responsibility we have toward each other. Moreover, the charge to carry out this task is not set upon the nations of the world nor their leaders nor upon a Supreme Being to hand us as though it were a gift. Rather, it is up to each and every one of us within the realm of our individual lives to make this dream come true.

Leave for a while the narrow sphere of your concerns, and with Israel's ancient seers ascend the mount of vision. Thence behold the millions of your fellow beings madly struggling for air and light, and a place in the sun. . . . You will forget your small cares in the woes of the defeated and helpless multitudes. The pang of compassion will grip your heart. . . . Then descend into the valley where men are struggling. Thither take the vision, the pang and the prayer, and transmute their urge into deeds of love.

—Mordecai Kaplan

If someone comes to you and asks your help, you shall not turn him off with pious words, saying: "Have faith and take your troubles to God!" You shall act as if there were no God, as if there were only one person in all the world who could help this man—only yourself.

—Reb Moshe Leib

Indeed, creating a climate where peace, harmony, and under-standing among all peoples exists is the very essence of what it means to be a Jew. Our most revered Jewish scholar put it this way:

> *What is hateful to you, do not do to your neighbor; this is the whole Torah. The rest is commentary; go and study.*
>
> —*Hillel*

Yet, given the imperfect world we live in, is it realistic to de-mand of ourselves that we strive for what may be nothing more than a utopian dream? And in light of our history, would it not be foolhardy to be anything but suspicious of those around us? A balance is obviously required and this is up to each individual to make. But let there be no mistake, the goal of achieving peace and harmony remains and to be a Jew requires nothing less than to continue to work for it.

How do we do this—especially in the shadow of the Shoah? Let us look at two Jews who have little in common other than their Jewishness. One was a scholar and philosopher who emigrated from Germany to Palestine and died at the age of eighty-seven two decades after the Holocaust; the other was an adolescent who did not live past her teens, succumbing days before Bergen-Belsen was liberated but whose haunting words lived on in her diary as an inspiration for future generations. Yet despite their differences, be-cause they both were Jews, their words contain the same message:

> *Let us dare, despite all, to trust!*
>
> —*Martin Buber*

> *In spite of everything, I still believe people are really good at heart.*
>
> —*Anne Frank*

CHAPTER
13

Jews Prize the Individual

It is said that when Rabbi Zusya, one of the early masters of Hasidism, died in 1800, he uttered this just before passing away:

In the world to come I shall not be asked: "Why were you not Moses?" I shall be asked: "Why were you not Zusya?"

Once again, as with most of our values, the importance placed upon the worth of the individual and the need to remain true to oneself, is something which has its roots in our earliest history and moves steadfastly forward—commencing with Abraham, who would not pay homage to idols because his inner voice bade him otherwise; to Hillel, who withstood the Roman torture of having his skin flayed rather than betray his individual belief; to Mordecai, who refused to bow to Haman because it ran afoul of Jewish tradition and the Second Commandment; to the wizened Hasid, who spat in the face of his Nazi oppressor knowing it would mean a cruel death; to those Jews, who would not betray their friends and co-workers at the McCarthy hearings and were blacklisted for adhering to their own code of morality rather than the "law" of the land.

Why do you suppose so many of the world's greatest minds have been Jewish? For example, despite our minuscule numbers,

Jews are prominent when the list of the most profound thinkers and contributors to the twentieth century are enumerated with Freud and Einstein generally at the top. It's not that Jews are necessarily smarter than most, but rather because of the emphasis we place upon independent thinking that encourages one to sometimes ponder in radical and amazing ways. Consider what Bruno Bettelheim said to Wayland Academy's graduating class in 1973:

> *When Einstein and Freud entered college they started out with no more than what each of you can bring to your college career; all they had to go on was the conviction that the creative mind of one single person can revolutionize the field he makes his own, and because of that, the whole world.*

To stand in the Jewish tradition means to serve no authority inconsistent with one's dreams, aspirations, and sense of right and wrong while recognizing the right of every other person to do likewise. But this is much easier said than done. There is, at best, a tension between the individual and the commonwealth in a free society, and in totalitarian regimes, one may face imprisonment, persecution, and even death as the price to pay to live by this value of ours. Nonetheless, we Jews still strive to respond to our individualism because the alternative is unacceptable.

> *I want to change my life before it changes me in ways I don't want to be changed.*
>
> —Bernard Malamud

> *In the beginning, I thought I could change man. Today, I know I cannot. If I still shout today, if I still scream, it is to prevent man from ultimately changing me.*
>
> —Elie Wiesel

> *Hell is trying to do what you can't do, trying to be what you're not.*
>
> —Anzia Yezierska

> *If you play a role long enough, there comes a point where the role begins to play you.*
>
> —Paul Krassner

We Jews can be an exacting lot. There is an accountability inherent in our Jewish system of values which requires you to be true to yourself. Sounds somewhat strange, doesn't it? Most systems of belief demand allegiance to a higher authority but Jews enjoin you to be yourself!

> *I didn't ask you what you do, but who you are.*
>
> —Elie Wiesel

> *He who is untrue to his own cause cannot command the respect of others.*
>
> —Albert Einstein

It would seem that gazing at the world through Jewish eyes means seeing the countless numbers of individuals in the way one observes snowflakes. It is said that no two snowflakes are alike and each has its own special beauty. To ignore the innate worth of each person's uniqueness goes against the grain of being a Jew. To be true to your "self"—your singularity—is the only way to lead a fulfilling and meaningful life.

> *Each individual should have the opportunity to develop the gifts which may be latent in him.*
>
> —Albert Einstein

> *Each of us has need of the personal confirmation that can come only when we know our "calling"—our existence in the fullest sense of the term. . . . We need to feel our work is "true". . . . Each one of us must risk ourself to establish ourself as the person that we are and risk failing in so doing.*
>
> —Maurice Friedman

> *Essence—by this I mean that for which a person is peculiarly intended, what he is called to become. There are great moments of existence when a man discovers his essence or rediscovers it on a higher plane; when he decides anew to become what he is and to establish a genuine relation to the world.*
>
> —Martin Buber

You feel so much better about yourself when you do what you think is the right thing.

—*Bruno Bettelheim*

We Jews value our individuality. It's part of what makes us who we are!

CHAPTER
14

Freedom, Equality, and Justice

Proclaim liberty throughout the land unto all the inhabitants thereof.

—Leviticus 25:10

Perhaps because Jews have been persecuted for thousands of years in a thousand different ways, we are sensitive to the importance of extending equality and justice to everyone. But without freedom, equality and justice are forever elusive and freedom is sometimes hard to come by. Hence, often against overwhelming odds, our history is filled with those of us who have fought for freedom.

The Exodus from Egypt—the flight from Pharaoh's despotism—is unique in that freedom came with God's intervention. Of course, there are those of us who would rather credit the man Moses with leading this first rebellion against tyranny. But the Exodus aside, all our struggles for freedom were undertaken by Jews much like you and me who would not live one day longer under the yoke of oppression.

Judah Maccabeus led our people in the battle against their Syrian tyrants and history credits this as the first insurrection for religious liberty. The revolt against Rome spanned a period of one hundred and fifty years, one of the longest in Roman history, and resulted in the destruction of the second temple in Jerusalem. During this time, the defenders of the fortress at Masada resisted Roman legions for three years before taking their own lives, preferring death to slavery.

The final in this series of rebellions against Rome was led by Rabbi Akiba and the young warrior Bar Kochba. In the end, Bar Kochba and Rabbi Akiba were executed and the remaining Jewish population was expelled from the land, commencing what has come to be known as the Diaspora.

Facing even more insurmountable odds, the Warsaw Ghetto's beleaguered population engaged the Nazis in an insurrection enduring six months. Appropriately enough, the uprising began on April 19, 1943, the first day of Passover. Mordecai Anielevitch, the 24 year old commander, wrote on that day:

> The dream of my life has come true. I have had the good fortune to witness Jewish defense in the Ghetto in all its greatness and glory.

There was another unlikely Jewish hero during World War II—a young woman by the name of Hannah Shenesh. After escaping the Nazis, she returned as a British paratrooper only to be recaptured and executed. She wrote her comrades:

> Continue on the way, don't be deterred. Continue the struggle till the end, until the day of liberty comes. . . .

But humans can be restrained by bonds more subtle than those of a despotic ruler or conquering nation. Without freedom from hunger and the ability to put sufficient food on the table for one's family, everything else becomes secondary.

It is no coincidence, therefore, that Jews were at the vanguard of the early labor movement. In 1934, the Jewish Labor Committee was founded by David Dubinsky, Adolf Held, and Charney Vladek. That year, responding to the growing persecution of Jews in Germany, Vladek, the managing editor of the Jewish *Daily Forward*, said:

One of the most important reasons why all tyrants hate us is because of our long experience in resisting injustice and cruelty. Over four thousand years ago a Jew by the name of Moses led the first great strike of bricklayers at the Pyramids, and since then all Pharaohs are our enemies.

More ethereal still, but perhaps of even greater importance, is to obtain freedom for the mind and soul—what one thinks, believes, and says. Jews have always striven for this, possibly the most precious of all freedoms.

It is imperative that freedom of judgment should be granted, so that men may live together in harmony, however diverse, or even openly contradictory, their opinions may be. In proportion as the power of free judgment is withheld, we depart from the natural condition of mankind.

—Baruch Spinoza

I believe in freedom, in man's right to be himself, to assert himself and to fight all those who try to prevent him from being himself. But freedom is more than the absence of violent oppression. It is more than "freedom from." It is "freedom to"—the freedom to become independent; the freedom to be much, rather than to have much, or to use things and people.

—Erich Fromm

We who lived in concentration camps can remember the men who walked through the huts comforting others giving away their last piece of bread. They may have been few in number, but they offer sufficient proof that everything can be taken from a man but one thing: the last of the human freedoms—to choose one's own way. It is this spiritual freedom—which cannot be taken away—that makes life meaningful and purposeful.

—Viktor Frankl

In the pursuit of equality and justice, it follows that freedom is something Jews seek for all people—not just for themselves. As the Israeli writer Amos Oz wrote:

Within Judaism, there has always been a powerful conviction that all men are created equal before God.

This has been put yet another way by Kinky Friedman, a Jewish country/western singer and novelist:

Goodman, Schwerner, and Cheney were three young civil rights workers who were killed by the Klan in Mississippi in the early sixties. Cheney was black, but Goodman and Schwerner were two Jewish kids from Queens . . . who went down South in the cause of freedom and equality. Abbie Hoffman, too, was down in Mississippi at about that time, and the civil rights movement, it should be noted, was generously infused with Jewish blood. . . . This is not really surprising for the dangerous role of the troublemakers in history has often fallen to the Jewish people.

In disproportionate numbers, Jews have been present in almost every organization contending against persecution and inequality from Amnesty International to groups promoting a woman's right to choose to gay rights and animal rights. At times, our demand for equality and freedom gives rise to a tension and the need to re-examine or even challenge some of our own Jewish ways—especially those which have ossified.

Consider what the author and professor, Shelley Fisher Fishkin, wrote in her adult bar/bat mitzvah class:

We will not allow women to be erased from our people's present and future, as women were so often erased from the record of our people's past. We are committed to preventing Judaism from inflicting that pain on others. We recognize that female and male, gay and straight, white and black, hearing and deaf, are all needed—for the repair of the world.

Jews are charged to bring the battle for freedom, justice, and equality to wherever it may take them—even to the gates of heaven. Unlike other peoples, there is no "off limit" sign barring Jews from decrying the denial of freedom.

According to the Talmud, a voice from heaven should be ignored if it is not on the side of Justice.

—Isaac Bashevis Singer

Only among the Jews does a man [Job] rage against God's injustice, demand a divine response, and receive that response. Only among the Jews is protest divinely sanctioned. Only among the Jews does this tormented insistence on justice seem to run as a central thread.

—Alicia Ostriker

For millennia, Jews have struggled for freedom and no one knows better than us that the effort is never-ending. Yet, we must never flinch from taking up the challenge this presents. In the Jewish tradition of "tikkun"—repairing the world, we will hopefully make life better for all.

This has been eloquently phrased by two Jews who sat on the Supreme Court of the United States:

When men know they might be free and equal, they will strive to be free and equal. When men have reason to hope for freedom and equality, they will sacrifice for it. And both the knowledge and the hope are alive on this earth, more alive now, perhaps, than ever before. The wind of change blows strongly, promising a new day, a new order, and a new life in the history of the world.

—Arthur Goldberg

Freedom is an unremitting endeavor, never a final achievement.

—Felix Frankfurter

CHAPTER
15

Love

Unlike the values discussed in the preceding chapters, which I suggest go to the heart of being a Jew and help define our identity, Jews have no monopoly on love. And yet, Jews do have a rather special way of looking at love which many of us sometimes take for granted or about which we may not even be aware.

Most of us are only remotely acquainted with Jewish mysticism, although in recent years with the growing popularity of adding a "spiritual" dimension to our lives, you may have become familiar with its teachings. This is something we'll be addressing in Part Five, but for now, I want to tell you how this aspect of our Jewish heritage deals with love—both in its carnal and ethereal sense.

Without going into greater detail, suffice it to say that according to Kabbalah, the inner and mystical aspect of Judaism, there is a female component of the Deity called the *Shekhinah* and a divine "sexual" coupling of sorts does take place. With this in mind, the influential sixteenth century Safed kabbalist, Moses Cordovero, wrote that sexuality between husband and wife is integral to the spiritual life and that "a man should be very careful to behave so that the *Shekhinah* cleaves always to him and never departs."

Thus, in addition to the emotional and romantic aspects of love, the physical element is crucial to the unity achieved in a marriage.

Taken together, this union between a man and a woman can sanctify life:

> *Only husband and wife together, united for life, bring the spirit of God, the spirit of holiness, into the home.*
> —*Rabbi Leo Baeck*

As we know from Chapter 9, the idea of "Oneness" is the foremost of our values and chief among our contributions to the world. In the Jewish tradition, the best way to achieve this is through love. Regardless of how you consider love—incorporating a spiritual or holy dimension, combining the sexual with the ethereal—we Jews view love so that in the end, a sense of "oneness" is reached.

> *When you love someone, you set yourself out of the way, and then you can be one with your lover. But, of course, no sooner is your self out of the way, then you are also one with yourself. No longer any illusion of some interior self set over against an exterior one.*
> —*Lawrence Kushner*

In Chapter 20, we'll talk about transience and eternity as part of Jewish spirituality. But for now, be advised that Jews behold love as something which never dies. No doubt, this is due in part because love aspires to the state of "Oneness" which, in turn, has to do with a Supreme Being or Life Force or that which links all living creatures—past, present, and future. Therefore, love is eternal.

While this has been expressed by many Jews over the centuries, I suggest it has never been more admirably articulated than by Anzia Yezierska, an immigrant who wrote stories reflecting her desperately poor life in the Jewish tenements of New York during the early part of the twentieth century. And yet, out of this destitute and frequently dispiriting milieu, she gives voice to the dreams of those about her as she dares to speak of the endlessness of love:

> *It's only we who die, but the spark of love, the flash of beauty from eye to eye, the throb from heart to heart goes on and on forever.*

Part IV

You Don't Have to Be Religious or Believe in God to Be Jewish

CHAPTER
16

God—Who's to Say?
Who's to "Know"?

From the very first moment when God revealed Him/Herself to Abraham, God withheld His/Her name from us Jews. In this fashion, God made it quite clear that it would not be possible to "know" God and while others may lay claim to this territory, Jews do not. To do otherwise would run counter to our rich heritage of iconoclasm and radical monotheism.

Hence, the word "God" is just that—a word pointing to something unfathomable and mysterious. Over the centuries and particularly in more recent years, scholars, theologians, and philosophers have come up with alternative appellations to substitute for "God" and I suppose I could use some of this nomenclature here, but I shall not. I prefer to retain the word "God."

One reason I do this is out of respect for tradition—something we Jews tend to have. Another reason has been eloquently expressed by Martin Buber: *We cannot cleanse the word "God" and we cannot make it whole; but defiled and mutilated as it is, we can raise it from the ground and set it over an hour of great care.*

So, if you prefer to think in terms of "Supreme Being," or "Eternal Thou," or "Ground of Being," or "Inner Light," or whatever terminology you like, know that I am meaning pretty much the same thing as we address the question as to whether you have to believe in God to be a Jew.

According to Sigmund Freud, early civilizations and thus their religions needed gods to alleviate man's sense of helplessness. These deities, he believed, served the function of exorcising the terrors of nature and reconciling humans to the cruelty of Fate, particularly death. Freud also theorized that since the father played a similar role to the child, the gods humans longed for were really a father-substitute and that "god is in every case modelled after the father . . . that god at bottom is nothing but an exalted father."

No doubt, if a list of the most famous atheists of all time were to be compiled, Freud would most certainly be at or near the top. In fact, one of his chief biographers, Peter Gay, wrote a book about Freud entitled *A Godless Jew*. But I submit what Freud actually did was to destroy a specific image of god—an anthropomorphic figure of the bearded old man in the sky who wields absolute power over us and in whose hands we lie like helpless children. While there are some who maintain this perception of God, which is clearly their right, there are also those of us for whom Freud desolated one more idolatrous vision of God, thus acting in the tradition of the foremost destroyer of idols, Abraham.

Over the years, and perhaps more today than ever, many Jews have held a healthy skepticism of the prevalent conception of God. You may be one of these Jews—some of whom search for other notions and beliefs about God going beyond the father figure:

> *For me, God is no longer a father figure. I'm not interested in what God looks like, but in how the world he created looks. I can read the thoughts of God from nature. The laws of creation interest me, and not whether God is made in the image of man with a long white beard, and has a son.*
>
> —*Albert Einstein*

> *Why do you address God by calling him Father? Who told you He is your father? Did He?*
>
> —*Rebbe Menakhem-Mendl of Kotzk*

*I noticed the other day that my onetime Father in Heaven has
dwindled to a weather-maker.*

—*Franz Rosenzweig*

If your images of God no longer suit you, do not hesitate to shed
them. And if you have already done so, this does not mean you are no
longer a Jew. Commencing a quest for God is something we Jews are
always taking up.

*In the search for the living God one must now and again destroy
the images that have become unworthy in order to create room for
a new one.*

—*Martin Buber*

*Everyone sought God, every race, every savage tribe. Mankind
could not exist without this search.*

—*Isaac Bashevis Singer*

Just where does one search for God and how does one go about
it? That's pretty much up to you. Consider this hasidic tale about
Rebbe Menakhem Mendle of Kotzk:

"Where is the dwelling of God?"
*This was the question with which the rabbi of Kotzk surprised
a number of learned men who happened to be visiting him. They
laughed at him: "What a thing to ask! Is not the whole world full of
His glory!"*
*Then he answered his own question: "God dwells wherever
man lets Him in."*

Or maybe, looking for God is like playing a game of hide-and-
seek as Elie Wiesel suggests in his book, *Somewhere A Master.*

*Rebbe Barukh's grandson, Yehiel, came running into his study in
tears.*
"Yekhiel, Yekhiel, why are you crying?"
"My friend cheats. It's unfair. . . . We played hide-and-

seek and I hid so well he couldn't find me. So he gave up; he stopped looking. And that's unfair.''

"God too, Yekhiel, is unhappy; He is hiding and man is not looking for Him. Do you understand, Yekhiel? God is hiding and man is not even searching for Him. . . .''

The danger does not exist in the search for God but in the complacency of adhering to an illusory image—one in which you no longer believe. Jews are prohibited from worshipping false gods and therefore, embarking on a quest for God, even one which never ends, is within the Jewish tradition.

Exactly where might such an exploration lead? Well, here are just a few examples from your fellow Jews who have struck out on their own. Although some lived centuries apart, it is interesting to note how similar they are in certain ways.

The foundation of all foundations, and the pillar of all wisdom, is to know that there is a First Existence, who brings all existence into being.

—Maimonides

I see a pattern. But my imagination cannot picture the maker of that pattern. I see the clock. But I cannot envisage the clockmaker. The human mind is unable to conceive of the four dimensions. How can it conceive of a God, before whom a thousand years and a thousand dimensions are as one?

—Albert Einstein

God is and acts solely by the necessity of His own nature; He is the free cause of all things. All things are in God, and so depend on Him, and without Him they could neither exist nor be conceived; lastly, all things are predetermined by God, not through His free will or absolute wish, but from the very nature of God or in finite power.

—Spinoza

Is there a God? Yes, there is. He is everything: the earth, the sky, the Milky Way, the crying of a child, the Nazi bomb, Einstein's theory, Hitler's Mein Kampf. *He is One. He is Eternal. My body is an infinitely small part of His body. My spirit is a drop in the ocean of His Spirit.*

—Isaac Bashevis Singer

It is true that everything contains something of the divine. But nothing looks like God, because God doesn't look like anything. There is simply nothing to see.

—Lawrence Kushner

Of course, one's search for God may turn up nothing. It is also possible that, like Freud, having nullified what is for you a spurious conception of God, you don't bother to undertake the search at all. You may have concluded there is no God or there once was a God but, to borrow Nietzche's phrase, "God is Dead." Yet, none of this means you stopped being a Jew.

There are those of us for whom personal tragedies or terrible events caused us to bury God. For some, God did not survive the Holocaust. Nowhere has this been more poignantly expressed than in Elie Wiesel's book, *Night*. Witnessing the hanging of another child, whom he describes had the face of "a sad angel," he heard someone behind him groan:

"Where is God? Where can He be now?" And a voice within me answered: "Where? Here He is—He has been hanged here, on these gallows."

The bottom line is that whether you believe or do not believe in God, or are simply uncertain about the matter, this should not affect your Jewish identity. If you consider yourself to be an atheist or an agnostic, you are in mighty fine company with other Jews, many of whom were ostracized or, as in the case of Spinoza, excommunicated.

Nor, should you allow your doubts about God to influence how you live your life. As we saw in Part Three, our Jewish values require we lead responsible and honest lives.

So, returning to the question whether you must believe in God to be a Jew, the answer is that you do not. Of course, you may believe in God and that is just as well. Perhaps it is like a character suggests in *Mr. Mani*, a novel by the Israeli writer, A.B. Yehoshua: *"No sir, a Jew is not required to believe in Him. As a rule, however, he does, since he has little else to believe in."*

Then again, as I hope you have learned by now, we Jews have a good deal to believe in which makes us who we are and enables us to proudly proclaim ourselves "Jews."

CHAPTER
17

Woe Is the Day Religion
Got "Organized"!

In my last semester at college, I took a course on Jewish existentialism taught by Maurice Friedman, translator and biographer of Martin Buber. Each student was assigned to choose one Hasidic tale that "spoke" to his or her "condition." I would like to share with you the tale I chose entitled, "The Crowded House of Prayer":

> *Once the Baal Shem stopped on the threshold of a House of Prayer and refused to go in. "I cannot go in," he said. "It is crowded with teachings and prayers from wall to wall and from floor to ceiling. How could there be room for me?" And when he saw that those around him were staring at him and did not know what he meant, he added: "The words from the lips of those whose teaching and praying does not come from the hearts lifted to heaven, cannot rise, but fill the house from wall to wall and from floor to ceiling."*

This tale about the founder of Hasidism spoke to me, because it reflected my perception of what was occurring in some synagogues where prayers were often recited by rote. "This is how I feel," I declared to the class. "And I will not enter a synagogue until there is authentic prayer going on inside."

Professor Friedman's eyes bore down on me and then he gently asked, "Why then, Richard, don't you go inside and help the others raise their prayers?"

My face flushed for I had no answer and the question had haunted me for many years until I finally found an answer. It's because I cannot lift my *own* prayers. I cannot pray. The notion of a deity to be worshipped and who hears my supplications is alien to me. How then, can I possibly lift anyone else's prayers?

Nonetheless, I still consider myself a Jew. It's just that no longer have I found synagogues conducive to expressing my "religious" emotions. Maybe you have felt this way also? If you have, you are not alone.

> *Religion becomes sinful when it begins to advocate the segrega-*
> *tion of God, to forget that the true sanctuary has no walls. . . .*
> *   —Rabbi Abraham Joshua Heschel*

> *Rabbi David Moshe told this story [The Sound of the Ram's Horn]*
> *about his father, Israel of Rizhyn:*
> *   The year he died, my father could no longer go to the House*
> *of Prayer. On New Year's Day I prayed with him in his room. His*
> *service was more wonderful than ever before. When he had*
> *ended, he said to me: "Today I heard the Messiah blow the ram's*
> *horn."*
> *   —Hasidic Tale*

> *Every day people are straying away from the church and going*
> *back to God. Really.*
> *   —Lenny Bruce*

Now, it may be you find synagogue a wonderful place that lends itself to spiritual sentiments within you and provides a satisfying experience. Or, you might believe synagogues serve a vital role in maintaining Jewish continuity. Possibly, you enjoy attending services as it is a time to be with family and friends or you regard the rabbi's sermons stimulating.

Whatever draws you to synagogue, that is all well and good. In Chapter 31, we'll explore the numerous and varied options you have regarding synagogue membership. But still, there are those of us, and perhaps you're one, who have not only been turned off by synagogues but, as a result, to all things Jewish.

Maybe what bothers you is something I call the "Edifice Complex," which runs rampant in almost all organized religions. This is the phenomenon resulting in the construction of imposing structures and the stifling of religious passion in many people. Moreover, it's not only the building which confines our spirited pursuit of religious sensitivity but its accompanying hierarchy as well.

Would it surprise you if I were to say you can be "religious" and yet never step foot inside a sanctuary or synagogue? Perhaps you won't be if you consider the following:

> *Professing religion does not mean being religious. Those concerned with religious experience, whether they are religionists or not, will not delight in seeing the churches crowded and in conversions. They will be the most severe critics of our secular practices and recognize that man's alienation from himself, his indifference to himself and to others, are the real threats to a religious attitude. . . .*
>
> *—Erich Fromm*

> *Religiosity is man's sense of wonder and adoration, an ever anew beginning. . . . Religion is the sum total of the customs and teachings articulated and formulated by the religiosity of a certain epoch . . . rigidly determined and handed down as unalterably binding. Once religious rites and dogmas have become so rigid that religiosity cannot move them . . . religion becomes uncreative and therefore untrue.*
>
> *—Martin Buber*

What I am saying is that you can be filled with "religiosity" but not adhere to any organized religion—which is what "Judaism" happens to be. This is the reason that throughout this book, I speak of being a Jew and being Jewish, and substitute "Jewishness" for "Judaism."

But again, I want to make it absolutely clear, if Judaism—the religion—works for you, that's great. However, for at least half of us American Jews, it isn't working and all I'm trying to get across is that this doesn't mean you're not a religious person and it certainly has nothing to do with your being a Jew!

Just because you are not observant of *halakhah* (Jewish Law), nor follow its ceremonies and rituals, nor have anything to do with Jewish prayer, is not to say you are not "religious" or "spiritual." Do you gaze at the world with wonder and awe? Do you have this sense of "Oneness" about which we spoke in Chapter 9? Do you approach the world and all that's in it with an openness and allow it to speak to you? If so, I submit you may be a more religious person than you think and what is more—a religious person in keeping with our Jewish way of viewing the world and responding to it.

Does the following ring true?

> *The most beautiful experience we can have is the mysterious. A knowledge of the existence of something we cannot penetrate, our perception of the profoundest reason and the most radiant beauty, which only in their most primitive forms are accessible to our minds—it is this knowledge and this emotion that constitute true religiosity; in this sense, and in this alone, I am a deeply religious man.*
>
> *—Albert Einstein*

The choice is yours. If Judaism and synagogue do not fulfill you, one option you have is to shrug your shoulders or glare with disdain at everything Jewish, including your own Jewish identity. "After all," you can say to yourself, "What is being a Jew other than following the canons of Judaism?"

On the other hand, you can recognize that not adhering to Judaism does not diminish your Jewishness. There are alternatives. You may search for the enigmatic entity we call "God." Or, if you wish, be a proud agnostic or atheist. You might want to embrace the esoteric wonder of "Life" as the Jew you are and go on from there. But whatever you decide, as we will see in the next chapter, what really matters is what you *do* in the world we live in that makes you a Jew.

CHAPTER
18

"Do as I Do—Not as I Preach"

Ever hear of Clara Lemlich? Chances are you haven't. During the early part of the twentieth century, Clara Lemlich lived in New York and was one of the more militant rank-and-file members of the ILGWU (International Ladies Garment Workers Union). In later years, she became a member of the Executive Board of the Women's Trade Union League and a suffrage organizer of the WTUL. But what really stood out about Clara Lemlich is that she was one of the most courageous women to have ever walked the face of this planet.

I must admit that until recently, I did not know who Clara Lemlich was, although my grandparents, David and Celia Bank, sure did. This is because at about the same time, my grandparents were also struggling to improve the plight of the average working man and woman in the garment industry where "sweat shops" were the norm as well as six day work-weeks and fourteen-hour days. Which is why my grandparents knew about Clara, who inspired twenty thousand workers to mount a general strike and demand recognition from the shirtwaist manufacturers.

Why am I telling you this? Sure, like so many of the early union activists, Clara Lemlich was Jewish, but there is more to her story than that. Let me explain.

Picture a hall packed with thousands of strikers. High upon the stage, Samuel Gompers himself had just finished his fiery oration. Before the next speaker could begin, a tumult arose from the throng and a small wiry woman was practically propelled toward the podium. Although she was not on the agenda, her battered and swollen face earned Clara the right to address the crowd. Her arms, neck, and shoulders were still fresh from the bruises and beatings inflicted upon her by the jailers at the Tombs, where she endured a two-week sentence for "disturbing the peace." Her crime? Walking the picket line while being pummeled by cops, thugs, and whores.

She spoke in Yiddish with simultaneous translations made into the diverse tongues of those present. All the union leaders combined couldn't hold a candle to the sway she held over that audience. In only a matter of minutes, Clara had the entire hall to its feet clamoring to strike until their goal was achieved.

Once order was restored, the chairman of the meeting asked those present to raise their right hands and promise to fight on until their union received full recognition. To seal their vow, he led them all—Jew and Gentile alike—in an adaptation of an old Hebrew oath. In unison, the crowd swore, "If I turn traitor to the cause I now pledge, if ever I forget thee, may my right hand wither." Unspoken, but in the hearts of many, were the Hebrew words meaning: "If I forget thee Jerusalem, may my right hand lose its cunning."

Clara Lemlich was a woman of action. She acted upon her beliefs, forged by values maintained over the centuries by her People. She set an example by what she did, not only what she said; and the price she paid (the brutality inflicted upon women strikers in the early days of the Labor movement was unimaginable), earned everyone's admiration.

Clara spoke in the language of her People—Yiddish. The values for which she fought—freedom and equality (recall Chapter 14)—were Jewish values. Clara did not recite platitudes. Nor did she pray and hope God would do something. Instead, Clara saw injustice and throttled it until she had beaten it to a pulp. And in this fashion, Clara Lemlich served as a model in the finest Jewish tradition—a true "woman of valor."

If someone comes to you and asks your help, you shall not turn him off with pious words, saying: "Have faith and take your troubles to

God!" You shall act as if there were no God, as if there were only one person in all the world who could help this man—only yourself.

—Rabbi Moshe Leib

When a man appears before the Throne of Judgment, the first question he is asked is not, "Have you believed in God?" or, "Have you prayed and observed the rituals?" He is asked: "Have you dealt honestly and faithfully in all your dealings with your fellow man?"

—The Talmud

For Jews, prayer and synagogue do not expiate wrongdoing committed upon fellow humans. Not even Yom Kippur can do this, as we shall see in Chapter 26. And while attending services can be a wonderful and meaningful experience also bolstering ethical conduct, it has never been meant as a substitute for being responsible to others and striving to maintain the values we Jews hold dear. To be a Jew requires nothing less.

Surely, it was the duty of all of us at least to look suffering in the eye.

—Amos Oz

It's not your guilt I want, but your responsibility.

—Arthur Miller

If I am not for myself, who is for me? And if I am for myself alone, what am I? And if not now, when?

—Hillel

CHAPTER
19

All Jews Are Humanists

One of the best commendations ever paid me occurred on my final day of classes as an undergraduate when a professor of mine, in making our good-byes, predicted I might be "the last of the great humanists." Or, at least I took it as a compliment.

Perhaps this is why I became perplexed whenever people vilified their opponents as "humanists." "What's wrong with that?" I wondered. Later, while touring the college circuit and addressing students at high schools, arguing against banning books like *To Kill a Mockingbird*, *The Catcher in the Rye*, *Of Mice and Men*, *The Adventures of Huckleberry Finn*, and, of course, *The Diary of Anne Frank*, I discovered what their detractors found objectionable was that these tomes promoted humanism. And again, I asked myself, "What's wrong with that?"

Although humanism is defined as "any system or mode of thought or action in which human interests, values, and dignity are taken to be of *primary* [emphasis added] importance," its opponents argue humanists are concerned *only* with people to the exclusion of everything else. These same critics allege humanists are the archenemies of everything worthwhile, i.e., God (religion), Mother (family values), and apple pie (country).

Now, I must confess that placing a high priority on humans (and nonhumans too), is rather important to me and, as you saw in Chapters 13 and 14, it provides the basis for some of our preeminent Jewish values. However, this is not to say humanism is exclusive of having spiritual beliefs.

In fact, there are all sorts of humanists as we shall see in Chapter 32. Some consider themselves "secular humanists," meaning any talk of religion and a Supreme Being is out of the question. Then, we have "religious humanists" who possess a spiritual component to their beliefs. For this latter group, in which I count myself, the following written by Martin Buber, expresses us well:

The prophets of Israel . . . have always aimed to shatter all security and to proclaim in the opened abyss of the final insecurity the unwished-for God who demands that His human creatures become real, they become human. . . .

Man cannot approach the divine by reaching beyond the human; he can approach Him through becoming human.

For Jews, being religious or reaching out to God is attained in the world in which we live. It is something we do as human beings with other human beings. In essence, this is what Hasidism was about when the movement began in the eighteenth century with the Ba'al Shem Tov rebelling against what he considered perfunctory, legalistic, and empty religious practices. Unfortunately, as with most religious movements, some have argued that Hasidism itself has now ossified and retreated into its own constricted world.

The thing is, whether you believe in God or a Supreme Being, hold spiritual thoughts, or are of the opinion that what you see is what you get, to be a Jew, you have no choice but to be a humanist. It's part of what being a Jew is.

What I'd like to do is put aside the different terms defining humanists and borrow a phrase coined by one of Abbie Hoffman's confederates, Paul Krassner—"practicing humanists." And we Jews, being "practicing humanists," venture out in the world applying our values in the only way we know—as human beings, with all our human frailties, for the benefit of other human beings.

If you've gotten this far along in this book, it is impossible not to reach this conclusion. But should you still have doubts, consider the following:

I have worshipped God in a variety of forms: childish, Hebrew, biblical, Homeric, natural, pantheistic, Platonic, Christian, and— atheistic. The business of man in this world is to be man.

                                    —Franz Rosenzweig

His mission was never to make the world Jewish but, rather, to make it more human.

                                       —Elie Wiesel

As we turn our attention in the next section to Jewish spirituality, do not forget that no matter how mystical or ethereal you may become, being Jewish means nothing less than living your life as a human being and feeling responsibility to all other living creatures at the same time.

Part V

Something Missing?
Try Jewish Spirituality!

CHAPTER
20

"Reality"—The Eternal Mystery

Spirituality and mysticism are deeply embedded in our Jewish tradition. There are many ways this can be approached, some of which we will cover in this part.

Perhaps one of the more well-known aspects of Jewish spirituality is Kabbalah (referred to in Chapter 9), which is the esoteric discipline of interpreting the Bible to penetrate its hidden meanings. But I do not treat Kabbalah here, although you are certainly welcome to do so and may want to read the books on this topic listed in the Appendix.

There are several reasons I omit this aspect of Jewish mysticism. First and foremost, I am no authority on this complex subject. Perhaps even equally important is that although Kabbalah is enjoying a surge in popularity, especially among nonobservant Jews, and Kabbalah centers are sprouting around the country attracting the rich and famous and even Gentiles, it is a system designed to provide explanations when explanations are not what I have in mind. The way I see it, and I'm not alone on this issue, we are dealing with questions where the answers are ultimately beyond our grasp. Finally, Kabbalah has its own conventions while I believe a different approach is called for—much like the character in Amos Oz's novel, *Fima*, who ponders:

There is no such thing as a universal map of reality; it simply cannot exist. Everyone has to find his own way somehow through the forest. With the help of unreliable inaccurate maps that we are born wrapped in or that we pick up here and there along the way.

While Kabbalah is something you may wish to pursue, I propose another option for your consideration if you are seeking a spiritual component to your Jewishness. Once again, I return to our beginning—to the times of Abraham, the great iconoclast.

It has been said that our belief system could have only come about in the desert. The Hebrews were a nomadic people, unfettered and free to roam the vastness of the stretching sands. When they laid their heads down at night—there was no roof above, only the starry sky. Nor were there walls to confine them nor sounds to interfere with the voice of God. Their thoughts were free to imagine and their minds open to receive and reflect on the world around them.

Could Abraham have heard God over the tumult of today's world? Above the din of the cars and trucks and sport utility vehicles whizzing by? Would he have been cognizant of God's prodding amidst the pandemonium of the car phones and cell phones and the faxes and the raspy voice of your computer screeching, "You've got mail!"

So I suggest you try as best you can to replicate the conditions in which the spiritual aspect of Jewishness arose. Which is precisely what Rabbi Zalman Schacter-Shalomi did when he found his life "bustling with activity" and something "unknown" stirring in his depths. Undertaking a forty-day retreat in "solitude, praying, meditating, writing, studying, and taking long walks," Schacter-Shalomi emerged to became one of the foremost leaders of the movement to imbue contemporary Jewishness with spirituality.

Now, I am not saying you must engage in a forty-day retreat. But while you may be unable to totally block out the clamor of your environment, you can try. And you can proceed as Abraham did by holding no "idols" before you, having no preconceptions, and opening yourself to the multifarious wonders of the world.

This is something Jews have done for millennia and I'd like to share some of their thoughts which are meant to be starting points for you. For example, consider how some Jews view the question of eternity:

> *The human mind cannot be absolutely destroyed within the body, but there remains of it something which is eternal.*
>
> *—Spinoza*

> *"I heard a nice little story the other day," Morrie says. "The story is about a little wave, bobbing along in the ocean, having a grand old time. He's enjoying the wind and the fresh air until he notices the other waves in front of him, crashing against the shore. 'My God this is terrible,' the wave says. 'Look what's going to happen to me!' Then along comes another wave . . . and it says to him, 'Why do you look so sad?' The first wave says, 'You don't understand! We're all going to crash! All of us waves are going to be nothing! Isn't it terrible?' The second wave says, 'No, you don't understand. You're not a wave, you're part of the ocean.'"*
>
> *—Morrie Schwartz from Tuesdays With Morrie*

> *How is it possible that someone should simply vanish? How can someone who lived, loved, hoped, and wrangled with God and with himself just disappear? I don't know how and in what sense but they're here. Since time is an illusion, why shouldn't everything remain?*
>
> *—Isaac Bashevis Singer*

> *Think about infinity. Time stretches backward for all eternity. And, if time infinitely stretches backward, must not everything that can happen have already happened? Must not all that passes now have passed this way before? And if everything has passed before in time's infinity—must not this moment have come before?*
>
> *What is immortal is this life, this moment. There is no afterlife, no goal toward which this life points, no apocalyptic tribunal or judgment. This moment exists forever.*
>
> *—Irvin Yalom*

When I read the above excerpt from Irvin Yalom's novel, *When Nietzsche Wept*, the words resonated within me since it mirrored what I had been contemplating for a number of years. The way I had begun to see things, since Einstein had established time and space are relative and time is not linear, any given minute is immortal. Thus, eternity becomes a by-product of time. The two are inextricably intertwined.

Yalom is a psychiatrist who toyed with time in a novel and likewise, Alan Lightman, a physicist, tinkered with time in a similar fashion in his novel, *Einstein's Dreams*:

> *Suppose time is a circle, bending back on itself. The world repeats itself, precisely, endlessly. And just as all things will be repeated in the future, all things now happening happened a million times before.*

American Jewish writers of fiction have also grappled with time and eternity. In the sequel to *Catch 22*, Joseph Heller writes in *Closing Time*:

> *From the physicists on the phone, Yossarian also thought that he heard, without understanding any of it, that in the world of science time continuously ran backward or forward, and forward and backward, and that particles of matter could travel backward and forward through time without undergoing change. Why then, couldn't he?*

While Saul Bellow phrases it succinctly: *The psyche has a different calendar.*

Since Jewish tradition focuses upon the here and now and what we do with it, as we shall see in Chapter 23, the actions you take in your life should not be affected by whether or not a moment in time is eternal. On the other hand, you may find it spiritually fulfilling to believe that what you are creating in any given fragment of time will last forever.

> *The transitoriness of life cannot destroy its meaning because nothing from the past is irretrievably lost. Everything is irrevocably stored. Whatever we have done or created, whatever we have learned and experienced—all of this we have delivered in to the past. There is no one, and nothing, that can undo it.*
>
> —*Viktor Frankl*

CHAPTER
21

The Soul

What would you say if I told you that of all people, the "Godless Jew" himself, Sigmund Freud, believed in the existence of a soul? No kidding, he did! Granted, Freud's perception of a soul did not imply immortality. Instead, he saw it as the part of a person that is most valuable while he or she is alive—one's essence. The distinguished educator and psychoanalyst, Bruno Bettelheim, points out that in his body of work, Freud repeatedly employed the German word "Seele" which properly translated would be "soul." His English translators, though, had preferred to use "mental" or the "mind" in order to retain a scientific dignity for the fledgling movement of Psychoanalysis, thus making it more palatable to the American medical and scholarly communities.

What is more, Freud believed the soul of one person could communicate with that of another:

> *Everyone possesses in his own unconscious an instrument with which he can interpret the utterances of the unconscious of other people. The unconscious of one human being can react upon that of another, without passing through the conscious.*

Clearly, there is nothing religious or divine about what Freud had in mind. Yet, some scholars have suggested Freud was influenced by Kabbalah, and indeed, there are similarities between Psychoanalysis and Kabbalah. For example, Edward Hoffman, who holds his doctorate in psychology, observes in his book, *The Way of Splendor*:

The kabbalists visualize several interrelated levels of consciousness or "souls." Our lowest desires urge us to fulfill instinctual needs. These innate animalistic drives are by necessity very powerful. But, the Kabbalah adds, we are also born with a transcendent self that yearns to rise above our petty wants. Moreover, to some kabbalists, we also comprise even more exalted cognitive aspects. These are said to lie almost wholly dormant during our day-to-day existence. Thus, throughout our lifetime, we experience an ever-present struggle among the different parts of our personality.

This sounds similar to the psychoanalytic structure of the mind where the Id and the Superego are perpetually waging war while the Ego constantly strives to strike a balance. And yet, I don't think there is much to be made of the proposition that Freud's theories were shaped by Jewish mysticism. In any event, it's too convoluted to get into here.

However, some psychoanalysts, like Viktor Frankl, do see a spiritual component to the human psyche:

Spiritual phenomena may be unconscious or conscious; the spiritual basis of human existence, however, is ultimately unconscious. Thus the center of the human person in his very depth is unconscious. In its origin, the human spirit is unconscious spirit.

I discuss Jews like Freud, Frankl, Hoffman, and Bettelheim, who studied the human psyche from a scientific and rational approach and concluded there is a soul, in order to make you aware that you do not have to be into Kabbalah or Jewish mysticism or be religious to have your Jewishness infused with spirituality. You can be a secular Jew or even an atheist. So feel free to open yourself to the possibility there is a soul inside you and every other living creature as well.

Nonetheless, much of what is spiritual belongs to the wing of Judaism encompassing Kabbalah and Jewish mysticism. Therefore, if it's spirituality you want, this bears further investigation.

The way the kabbalists regard the soul is succinctly stated by Areyh Kaplan in *Meditation and Kabbalah*:

Man consists of matter and form, body and soul. The soul con-stantly has a burning desire to attach itself to God. It is enveloped by a physical body, however, which acts as a barrier to such attachment.

Freud's notion of one person's unconscious communicating with the unconscious of another finds a more phantasmal and aes-thetic parallel in Hasidism which expresses much the same thing about the interaction between two souls:

When two people meet, it is two souls against one body. Because bodies are self–centered by nature, they cannot join forces—each pursuing its own physical needs. Souls, however, are selfless by nature, so when two people join forces, their souls converge.
—Rabbi Menachem Mendel Schneerson

From every human being there arises a light that reaches straight to heaven and when two souls that are destined to be together find each other, their streams of light flow together, and a single brighter light goes forth from their united being.
—Baal Shem Tov

I particularly like the saying from Hasidism's founder, the Ba'al Shem Tov, and I think it makes a wonderful addition to a wedding ceremony. It lends credence to the idea that the bride and groom have found "soul mates" in each other.

The Ba'al Shem Tov's adage also reflects Hasidism's basic premise that God's Presence of Divine Light shattered and splintered into a multitude of transcendent sparks and there exists in every-thing and every living creature one of those divine sparks. More-over, it is our task to gather these embers and bring them together for the redemption of the world. In *Hasidism and Modern Man*, Martin Buber explains it this way:

> *All souls are one; for each is a spark from the original soul, and the whole of the original soul is in each.*

Contrary to Freud and those like him, there are those who believe in the immortality of the soul. Here are two ways it has been expressed:

> *He [a recently departed man] is even more present than during his lifetime, since his soul is freed from the physical constraints of time and space.*
> *The soul never ages, it only becomes more vibrant.*
> —Rabbi Menachem Mendel Schneerson

> *There is no such thing as an old man. An old man is just an old little boy. I keep making plans as though I will live forever. Perhaps this is a proof that the soul is immortal.*
> —Isaac Bashevis Singer

Whether the soul is eternal or transient, I leave to you. And you certainly do not have to believe in the existence of a soul to be Jewish. However, the concept of a soul is well established along the full array of Jewish tradition and among all sorts of Jews—although, like everything else about us Jews—there is no uniform opinion regarding it.

CHAPTER
22

For Jews Life Is Meaningful
and Sacred

There must have been times in your life when you have wondered, "Just what is it all about?" "Does Life have a purpose?" "Is there any more to my existence than being one more fleeting speck of dust in the vast cosmos?"

Chances are, these are questions you contemplated as an adolescent or young adult, perhaps as a college student. But then you "grew up" and came to accept things as they are so you buried them away with other "youthful" reflections. Or, possibly these questions continue to gnaw at you and you wrestle with them still.

I think that sometimes our cerebral constitution makes us Jews more disposed to such introspection. And since questioning everything is part of our radical monotheism and iconoclastic nature, Jews are prone to set their sights and minds upon weighty subjects such as existence and the Universe and our individual place therein and then ask, "What gives?"

But this is no reason to find yourself staring at a blank and desolate wall concluding like Nietzsche (who wasn't Jewish), that God is dead, or opting for the nihilistic existentialism of Sartre (distinguishable from our own brand of existentialism which we'll discuss in the next Chapter). In fact, the Jewish response to whether there is meaning to "life" and does an individual's existence have any significance, is a resounding "Yes!" Despite thousands of years of persecution, pogroms, exile, and ultimately the Shoah, the Jewish answer is an affirmation of life and of every human being.

To be sure, discerning the meaning of life is no small task. Navigating our individual journeys through life's waters can be difficult, if not treacherous.

> The way in this world is like a knife's edge. There is an abyss on either side, and the way of life lies in between.
> —Rabbi Moshe Leib of Sasov

But like everything else in our Jewish heritage, it is up to you to chart your own course and proceed under your own power. The wherewithal lies within you.

> As the hand held before the eye conceals the greatest mountain, so the little earthly life hides from the glance the enormous lights and mysteries of which the world is full, and he who can draw away from behind his eyes, as one draws away a hand, beholds the great shining of the inner worlds.
> —Rabbi Nachman of Bratzlav

The Jewish emphasis has always been on the individual. Not only does this mean your individual life but also the life of every other living creature. Each life is laden with meaning—ultimate meaning. This has never been expressed more eloquently and with greater simplicity than in the Talmud:

> He who saves a single life, it is as though he has saved the entire world.

If it's life's meaning you're after, you won't find it gazing in awe at the multitude of stars, or sequestering yourself in a trancelike state in a room, or pondering one philosophical paradigm after another. Jewish spirituality is not something that occurs in a vacuum or ivory tower or cloister and therefore, it's not likely you'll find life's meaning in such places. Instead, pick yourself up and with the uniqueness that is you, go out in the world and encounter life.

Moreover, only you, and no one else, can determine what that answer will be.

> *For the meaning of life differs from man to man from day to day and from hour to hour. What matters, therefore, is not the meaning of life in general but rather the specific meaning of a person's life at a given moment. One should not search for an abstract meaning. Each man is questioned by life; and he can only answer to life by answering for his own life. . . .*
>
> *The answer to the question "What is the meaning of life?" can only be given out of one's whole being—one's life is itself the answer to the question of meaning.*
>
> *—Viktor Frankl*

> *Only he reaches the meaning who stands firm, without holding back or reservation, before the whole might of reality and answers it in a living way. He is ready to confirm with his life the meaning he has attained.*
>
> *—Martin Buber*

Jews do not simply set out on a mission to discover life's meaning. It's not to be found under some rock. Not only will your actions determine whether you'll arrive at an answer but your lived life will actually help shape what that answer will be.

Purely as a point of departure and for you to mull over, here is how other Jews have looked upon this matter:

> *It is entirely conceivable that life's splendor forever lies in wait about each one of us in all its fulness, but veiled from view, deep down, invisible, far off. It is there, though, not hostile, not reluctant, not deaf. If you summon it by the right word, by its right name, it will come.*
>
> *—Franz Kafka*

> *This, then, is an insight we gain in acts of wonder: not to measure meaning in terms of our own mind, but to sense a meaning definitely greater than ourselves.*

On the certainty of ultimate meaning we stake our very lives. Life would come to naught if we acted as if there were no ultimate meaning.

—Abraham Joshua Heschel

The good life, in Freud's view, is one that is full of meaning through the lasting, sustaining, mutually gratifying relations we are able to establish with those we love, and through the satisfaction we derive from knowing that we are engaged in work that helps us and others to have a better life.

—Bruno Bettelheim

The ideals which have lighted my way have been Kindness, Beauty, and Truth. Without the sense of kinship with men of like mind, without the occupation with the objective world, the eternally unattainable in the field of art and scientific endeavors, life would have seemed to me empty. The trite objects of human efforts—possessions, outward success, luxury—have always seemed to me contemptible.

—Albert Einstein

Spirituality, and in particular Jewish spirituality, has to do with things other than the material. This is where Einstein hangs his hat—or should I say his socks that he rarely wore. Ever since our nomadic meandering over deserts and carrying only what possessions were necessary, it has always been part of our Jewish baggage to strive for a higher level of existence going beyond bricks and mortar and worldly goods that confine our actions and limit our visions.

Perhaps now that you're thinking about it, you may be feeling more than a little discomfort, like Sammy Singer, a character in Joseph Heller's *Closing Time*, who bemoaned:

I missed out on much, and that now that I no longer have it, mere happiness was not enough.

While there is nothing wrong with being happy, or having a nice house and car, nonetheless, it may be you no longer deem this to be sufficient and you are left with an emptiness inside. Possibly you desire a more fulfilling existence. If so, why not try our distinct brand of Jewish spirituality which has woven its way through the millennia with all sorts of Jews—Talmudic scholars and hasidic masters, novelists and poets, psychoanalysts and scientists—all engaged in living a more meaningful life in the Jewish tradition.

CHAPTER
23

Jews and Existentialism

Nothing exists. Nothing indeed does exist. Now listen. Nothing cannot exist alone. That's the whole crux of the matter. Nothing cannot exist alone. If nothing cannot exist alone, then something exists. And if something exists, then all the rest in the course of time will exist. Hence all of reality exists because nothing exists, but cannot exist alone.

Welcome to the world of existentialism. Or, more precisely, existentialism seen through the eyes of a Jew since the above was written by Henry Roth, author of *Call It Sleep*, in November 1963, several days after the Kennedy assassination. It was around that time when I was first exposed to existentialism and as I learned more about it, I found some aspects to be quite compelling.

Historically, existentialism is a fairly new movement with its formal beginnings in the mid-nineteenth century. Nietzsche, who was becoming popular in the sixties, was portrayed (not necessarily correctly) as an existentialist, and thus a melancholy cloud hung over the existentialist mood. Thus, it seemed to me, existentialism wasn't the most exhilarating philosophy to embrace.

But there is another side to existentialism that I hadn't considered then because it wasn't well known. I came upon it my senior year in college. Remember back in Chapter 17, I told you I took a course on Jewish existentialism and I shared with you one of the Hasidic tales which spoke to "my condition?" Well, that's when my interest in existentialism really began.

Now what, you may ask, has Hasidism to do with existentialism? Maybe not much regarding the Sartre and Kierkegaard brand but everything to do with Jewish existentialism.

Hasidism concerns itself with hallowing the everyday and particularly each moment. Which is precisely what being Jewish is all about and has been since its inception. Recall the last line of the quote I cited by Hillel in Chapter 18:

And if not now, when?

Well, that's Jewish existentialism in a nutshell. Hillel understood that every minute you are alive has an urgency to it. It is an opportunity to reach into eternity. Hillel was not alone in this belief.

All our seeming contradictions arise from the equation between the "today" that is a bridge to tomorrow, and the "today" that is a springboard to eternity. No day has written on its forehead which of the two "todays" it is. One can never tell.
                                                    —*Franz Rosenzweig*

In ecstasy all that is past and that is future draws near to the present. Time shrinks, the line between the eternities disappears, only the moment lives, and the moment is eternity.
                                                    —*Martin Buber*

The ultimate insight is the outcome of "moments" when we are stirred beyond words, of instant wonder, awe, praise and radical amazement. It is at the climax of such moments that we attain the certainty that life has meaning, that time is more than evanescence, that beyond all being there is someone who cares.
                                                    —*Abraham Joshua Heschel*

One does not have to agree with Rabbi Heschel that the magnitude of the moment infuses life with meaning and proves there is a Divine Being or God. This is what sets Heschel apart from most other existentialists in that he would be considered a "religious" existentialist. But as I said in Part Four, you don't have to be religious or believe in God to be Jewish. Likewise, you don't have to believe in God or be religious to be a Jewish existentialist.

Perhaps, you are of the opinion that each and every segment of time carries the potential for beauty and meaning and this, in and of itself, is enough. If so, know that there are many Jews who hold a similar outlook.

> Michael was about to ask him a very simple question, so simple that ordinarily men waste it, asking it without meaning: "Who are you?" He passed it over in silence. Pedro would have answered, "I am. Isn't that enough?"
>
> —Elie Wiesel

> I dispute the pessimistic poet's view that the transience of what is beautiful involves any loss in its worth. The beauty of the human form and face vanish forever in the course of our own lives, but their evanescence only lends them a fresh charm. A flower that blossoms only for a single night does not seem to us on that account less lovely.
>
> —Sigmund Freud

Freud calling the poet a "pessimist"? That's a switch, isn't it? But the fact is, Freud's appreciation for the opportunity to behold the radiance in every minute we are alive is what sets our brand of Jewish existentialism apart. It is meant to be uplifting and add a positive dimension to your life. But naturally, there's a catch.

I hate sounding like a broken record spinning the same old tune, but once again, it's up to you. As you have figured out by now, being a Jew means you're on your own. Don't look to God or the rabbi or your friends and family to hallow the moment for you. It's on you to do it in your own way. Because being a Jew means you must be a responsible and thinking and caring human being.

> The way of man is unique for each particular man because each man is unique and is in a unique situation. "This is now my way,—where is yours?"
>
> —Maurice Friedman

It did not really matter what we expected from life, but rather what life expected from us. We needed to stop asking about the meaning of life, and instead to think of ourselves as those who were being questioned by life—daily and hourly. Our answer must consist, not in talk and meditation but in right action and in right conduct. "Life" does not mean something vague, but something very real and concrete. . . . No situation repeats itself, and each situation calls for a different response.

—Viktor Frankl

I possess nothing but the everyday out of which I am never taken. The mystery is no longer disclosed. . . . I know no fulness but each mortal hour's fulness of claim and responsibility. Though far from being equal to it, yet I know that in the claim I am claimed and may respond in responsibility, and know who speaks and demands a response.

—Martin Buber

It is difficult to imagine how one can be a Jew and not be an existentialist. Being a Jew demands responsibility to each and every moment which presents itself to you as life unfolds. It can be beautiful and meaningful, or brutal and ugly. But it is this segment in time in which you are challenged and to which you are bound to respond. It is what you make of it and it can be everything.

Some things bear repeating. So, once again, turning to the great sage Hillel:

And if not now, when?

CHAPTER
24

Jews, Buddhism, and Meditation

Is this one of your worst nightmares? You are bustling through an airport terminal when a polite young man or woman with a shaved head presses a flower in your face and when gazing up to say "no thanks," you discover the *shayner* face is none other than your son or daughter. And so, you learn, your child is a Hare Krishna.

That would not be such an irrational anxiety, I'm afraid to say. While there are few hard statistics, it is believed Jews comprised a disproportionate percentage of Americans who embraced Buddhism in the second half of the last century. For example, it has been estimated that at one time, fifty percent of those practicing Zen in San Francisco and a third in Los Angeles were Jewish.

What motivates many of the Jews who turn to Buddhism is an opportunity to attain the spirituality they find lacking in Judaism. These Jews cringe at the formalities of synagogue services; the minutiae of Jewish law; and the required observances to remain a Jew in good standing. Hence thousands, indeed tens of thousands, have abandoned Judaism seeking a more spiritual life in Buddhism.

Yet, with many of these individuals, Jewish identity was never entirely discarded. In fact, there is a common appellation for Jewish Buddhists. They are often referred to as "JUBUs" and they consider themselves to be both Jewish and Buddhist. What is more, some of these "JUBUs" are proud of their Jewishness and Buddhism.

Consider what Ayyah Khema has to say on the subject. Ayyah was born and raised a Jew but when searching for a more spiritual way of living, she embraced Buddhism. After the death of her husband, Ayyah received ordination as a Buddhist nun. When asked about being Jewish, she replied, "Of course I'm still Jewish. What else could I be? Jewish is something you *are*, and I am proud of our heritage."

Indeed, some "JUBUs" believe they are better Jews because of their Buddhism. For example, Sylvia Boorstein, author of *That's Funny, You Don't Look Buddhist*, writes:

> *I am a Jew because my parents were mild-mannered, cheerful best friends who loved me emotionally and they were Jews. I am a prayerful, devout Jew because I am a Buddhist. As the meditation practice that I learned from my Buddhist teachers made me less fearful and allowed me to fall in love with life, I discovered that the prayer language of "thank you" that I knew from my childhood returned. . . .*

Now, you don't have to become a Buddhist to learn meditation since this is part of our Jewish tradition, particularly among those engaged in Jewish mysticism and Kabbalah. Thus, if it's meditation you are after, you can pursue it from a uniquely Jewish perspective.

In addition to conferences and seminars that are advertised, there are a number of Jewish meditation centers around the country such as: **Sarah's Tent**, c/o Malibu Jewish Center & Synagogue, 24855 Pacific Coast Highway, Malibu, CA 90264, (310) 456-2178; and **Elat Chayyim**, 99 Mill Hook Rd., Accord, NY 12404, (800) 398-2630.

So, do you rend your clothing and declare your son or daughter an "apikoros" or dead to you if he or she follows Buddhism? Or, if you yourself begin contemplating what Buddhism has to offer, whether it be its spirituality or meditative techniques leading to a more tranquil existence, do you refrain from looking into it because you are afraid you won't be considered a Jew anymore?

Technically, Buddhism is not a religion because it does not focus on a Supreme Being, so some assert that it is no more incompatible with being Jewish than, say, being a Democrat or belonging to NOW or the ACLU. But ultimately, the answer depends upon how you define Jewishness and what it means to be Jew. If you embrace the more inclusive definitions of "Who is a Jew?" discussed in Part Two, I submit there is nothing inconsistent about incorporating Buddhism into your life and remaining a Jew.

The concepts of "Oneness" and respect for every living creature are shared by Jews and Buddhists alike. Meditation may be something you find very helpful in coping with the daily tumult with which we are frequently faced. And as for the spiritual element you may find missing in your life, well, if Buddhism provides it, why not go for it. You can still be a Jew.

But one thing should be clear as we conclude Part Five. If it's spirituality you want, you don't have to seek it from Buddhism. Nor must you study Kabbalah or become a hasid to attain it. These are options, but there are other alternatives that I hope you have learned in the preceding pages.

Jewish spirituality exists in many and varied forms from which you can choose. What is more, you can apply it in numerous ways in your life. For example, several opportunities to do this arise on a regular basis each and every year. They are our Jewish holidays— occasions which you can hallow and infuse with meaning and spirituality.

Let's see how we can do this and perhaps also determine why these days should be celebrated in the first place. On to Part Six. . . .

Part VI

How to Celebrate the Holidays and Why!

CHAPTER
25

There's No Place Like Home!

My wife hails from a large family on her mother's side. She had eight aunts and uncles and more cousins than I could keep track of. So it came without saying that when the clan gathered for holiday dinner—whether Rosh Hashanah or break the fast or a seder, kinfolk would be spilling from the dining room, into the hallways, and even out the door—weather permitting.

Yet, despite the tumult, a radiance pervaded the air. Everyone knew there was no more suitable way to spend the holiday. Nor, could there be a better place than the home to gather and commemorate the occasion.

Not that this implies you must have a large family. Size has nothing to do with it. Seders and holiday dinners while I was growing up were rather small affairs. But that didn't diminish the glow the candles reflected in the dining room window and the warmth in my chest as I recall those times.

The largeness of your family is not a factor in celebrating the holidays. Why, you can mark the event as part of what we now call the "nuclear" family, or perhaps with friends, or even by yourself. The point is that whatever it is you do and with whomever you do it—your home can be a wonderful place to carry it out.

Like so much else I consider to be "Jewish," this practice has its roots in our beginnings. The nomadic Hebrews had no permanent edifices to observe special days. But they did have their tents that traveled with them and where, with their *mishpocheh*, as well as any stranger who happened by, they would assemble to hallow the day.

The Temple in Jerusalem, both the first and second; the centers of learning and houses of worship in Babylon and other cities providing havens for Jews during the Diaspora; the small shuls of the shtetls; the imposing synagogues in Berlin, Vienna, and Warsaw; and the temples and synagogues you attended as children but today serve as churches even though the Star of David is still visibly etched in the masonry wall—all of these are gone. The immutability of such structures is an illusion. Yet, throughout the centuries, the home has remained the true center of the Jewish people. What more fitting a place to commemorate our festivals!

Observing a holiday in your home affords you an opportunity to be creative because it is up to you to prepare for the occasion. You can do this in your own way—culling from the cornucopia of Jewish customs and traditions, customizing them to suit your desires. You can even conceive of one or two ceremonies of your own. The most important thing is, no matter what you choose or how you celebrate, you carry it out in a manner which is meaningful to you and for those keeping the holiday with you.

As we proceed with the following chapters in Part Six, feel free to select and alter any of the suggestions made. That's all they are—like everything else offered in these pages—just some thoughts for you to mull over as you contemplate why and how to commemorate our Jewish holidays.

CHAPTER
26

Rosh Hashanah/Yom Kippur

Are you familiar with the Sholem Aleichem story, "A Yom Kippur Scandal"? It's possible you are and yet not know it because this tale has been recounted in different ways, frequently around the high holidays, and sometimes without giving credit to the great Yiddish storyteller. In any event, it goes something like this:

On the day before Yom Kippur, a Litvak found himself stranded in the town of Kasrilevke. No one knew much about this stranger other than he must be a wealthy and successful man the way he went around bestowing rubles on so many of the townspeople. So naturally, he was honored with a place at the Eastern Wall for the holiest of holy days.

The Litvak davened the entire day, never once taking a break for a breath of fresh air or even to relieve himself. Then, just as the service ended and the rabbi blessed everyone with *L'Shanah Tovah*, a guttural cry erupted from the throat of the distinguished visitor.

"I've been robbed! I've been robbed!" shrieked the Litvak, his face red as a beet. "Someone has made off with all my 1800 rubles! I couldn't leave such a sum in my room or carry it in my pocket here in synagogue so I left it under the praying stand and now . . . now it is gone!"

The rabbi and the entire congregation were mortified. The elders fell over one another making their way to the distraught guest. Once the commotion died down, all looked to the rabbi for a solution which was promptly forthcoming. The rebbe was not a tall man but he puffed himself up to make every bit of his five foot frame rise to the occasion as he proclaimed:

"No one is to leave the shul. Everyone must turn their pockets inside out and we will find the 1800 rubles and the guilty culprit. And on Yom Kippur yet!" The rebbe spat.

Within minutes, all pockets were emptied and a hundred palms turned upward in innocence, save one. In the very last row was slumped Lazer Yossel. His face was ashen and his shoulders trembled. In unison, all eyes in the congregation glared at poor Lazer, who could only gaze at his feet shuffling on the floor.

"Lazer!" the rebbe bellowed. "Empty your pockets, immediately!" Lazer sat in silence and shook his head. "Now!" thundered the rebbe.

"Anything but that, rebbe," Lazer pleaded. "I did not take the man's money."

"Then you have nothing to fear," said the rebbe. But Lazer still refused. A nod from the rebbe and a half dozen men grabbed Lazer, who was by then in tears, and turned him topsy-turvy spilling out the contents of his pockets—a gnawed chicken bone, some potato peelings, and a few bread crumbs. But no 1800 rubles.

The rabbi departed in shame that this should happen in his shul and on Yom Kippur, no less! The people of Kasrilevke spilled out from the shul in laughter, leaving the mortified Lazer Yossel on the back bench where he had been so ignominiously searched.

And what of the 1800 rubles stolen from the Litvak? It was gone and no one ever bothered to find out more about it.

There is a great deal of history and custom to this holiest day in the Jewish year. In biblical times, the high priest of the Temple purified the sanctuary and atoned ritually for the sins committed by the Israelites by symbolically placing them on a goat and driving it into the wilderness. Later, forgiveness from God was sought by prayers of penitence and fasting. Vows and contracts became subject to recision which proved very useful to the Marranos who publicly accepted Christianity in Spain but remained closet Jews. In fact, this is precisely what the *Kol Nidre* addresses.

Similarly, Rosh Hashanah has its own special implications. It commences the ten-day penitence period and marks the start of a new year. Suppliants ask God to be written in the Book of Life and during the service, the portion of the Bible is read that narrates Abraham's willingness to sacrifice Isaac, thus demonstrating his obedience to God.

Now possibly, like me, the conventional reasons for commemorating the high holy days just don't work for you. If this is the case, and you have no desire to attend synagogue, be assured there are equally compelling reasons, also very much in the Jewish tradition, to mark this time of the year.

Let's return for a moment to Lazer Yossel who ate on the sly during the Yom Kippur fast. The interesting thing is that he'd rather be accused of stealing from a fellow man than affronting God and violating the proscription of eating on the Day of Atonement. And not only Lazer but the rabbi and entire congregation quickly forgot about the crime committed upon the visiting Litvak. Thus, Lazer and the people of Kasrilevke, and I would venture to say many of us today, miss a whole other dimension behind the meaning of Yom Kippur.

You see, Lazer had it all wrong. As it is written in the Mishna that infractions against God are forgiven on the Day of Atonement, Lazer could have petitioned God to be pardoned for breaking the fast. But transgressions upon others are not excused until the aggrieved party has been appeased. The emphasis is to be responsible to your fellow human and other living creatures. Failure to do so is not mitigated by fasting or praying.

The prophet Isaiah spoke about the purpose of the fast and condemned the fact it was often sanctimoniously carried out.

Wherefore have we fasted, and Thou seest not?
Wherefore have we afflicted our soul, and Thou takest no knowledge?
Behold, in the day of your fast ye pursue your business,
And exact your labours.
Behold, ye fast for strife and contention,
And to smite with the fist of wickedness;

> *Ye fast not this day so as to make your voice to be heard on high. . . .*
> *Is not this the fast that I have chosen?*
> *To loose the fetters of wickedness,*
> *To undo the bands of the yoke, And to let the oppressed go free,*
> *And that ye break every yoke?*
> *Is it not to deal thy bread to the hungry,*
> *And that thou bring the poor that are cast out to thy house?*
> *When thou seest the naked, that thou cover him. . . .*
>   . . . *Isaiah 58:3–8*

Isaiah's admonishment rings as true today as when it was first exclaimed. Prayers and fasting are meaningless if perfunctorily performed. Sometimes, when the reason to fast eludes you, you should give it up as Elie Wiesel did at one point in his life—in Auschwitz.

> *Yom Kippur. The Day of Atonement. Should we fast? The question was hotly debated. To fast would mean a surer, swifter death. The whole year was Yom Kippur. But others said we should fast simply because it was dangerous to do so. We should show God that even here, in this enclosed hell, we were capable of singing His praises.*
>   *I did not fast, mainly to please my father, who had forbidden me to do so. But further, there was no longer any reason why I should fast. I no longer accepted God's silence. As I swallowed my bowl of soup, I saw in the gesture an act of rebellion and protest against Him.*
>   *And I nibbled my crust of bread. In the depths of my heart, I felt a great void.*

When my sons were growing up, I never asked either of them to fast on Yom Kippur. All I said was that if they had a reason to fast, then they should. And if they did choose to abstain from eating, I would ask them why.

Very often, I'd be told they fasted to know how poor people felt when there was not enough food. At other times, they would answer with a purpose similar to mine saying it helped to create an atmosphere conducive to contemplation and set the day apart.

There are many possible reasons you might abstain from eating. I particularly like what Mordecai Kaplan has to say about fasting:

*When we refrain from indulging our physical appetites for a lim-
ited period, in order to devote ourselves for a time exclusively to
demands that rank higher in our hierarchy of values, we are not
denying the physical appetites their just place in life; we are
merely recognizing the need of putting them in their place.*

Commemorating the high holy days connects you with the
history of our people and with Jews all over the world. What you do is
up to you, but how you do it is something else again. To borrow the
Hebrew term, *kavvanah*, you should be fully focused upon the day
and act in all sincerity. Consider this hasidic tale about the Ba'al
Shem Tov:

*The day after Yom Kippur, the Ba'al Shem Tov ordered his horses
and carriage to be made ready and told his driver to set off in the
direction of the forest. At an inn operated by a Jew, he stopped.*

*Upon entering the inn, the owner said, "Oh, Rabbi, I have
something terrible to confess." The Ba'al Shem Tov asked what this
was and the Jew went on with his explanation. "I live here in the
forest far away from other Jews. Once a year on Yom Kippur I
would like to pray together with other Jews, but somehow I have
not been able to do it. This year I was determined I would do it, and
we all started off for the city. But when we had gone a little way, I
remembered I had forgotten to close the back door. So I sent my
wife and children ahead, took a horse and rode back.*

*"While I was closing the back door, a customer came in the
front door, and while I was serving him, another came in and then
another and soon it was too late for me to go. I prepared to pray but
discovered the prayer books had gone with my family. Since I have
never learned Hebrew, all I could recite was the Hebrew alphabet.
So what I did was to stand up and face Jerusalem and I just recited
the alphabet and I said to God: 'Here God, here are your holy
letters, you put them into the right words. . . .'"*

*The Ba'al Shem Tov put his arms around the man and said, "It
was revealed to me in a vision that on this Yom Kippur your prayers
had opened the gates of heaven, and I came to you to find out how
to do it."*

The Ba'al Shem Tov recognized that this simple Jewish inn-
keeper followed his heart in hallowing the day and in doing so, cast

open the gates of Heaven. Nothing could be more consistent with being a Jew.

You have many options and activities from which to choose to mark the occasion. Perhaps, you opt for joining your fellow Jews in synagogue or in prayer groups or study groups. It may be that a gathering of the clan with a table spread of gefilte fish and matzo ball soup promotes the spirit you wish to attain. You might want to do some quiet reading or journal writing in the privacy of your study. Or, perhaps, sit and talk with others about issues beyond the everyday business which fills our lives. Maybe you wish to hear *Kol Nidre* being chanted and yet you don't want to attend services. Consider buying a CD or tape with Jewish music that contains this impassioned incantation.

I'll tell you my favorite activity. It began when my boys were still little. My wife and I would take them to a park or woods and just walk along and talk and be together. It was the commencement of my love affair with nature and over the years, this has become a regular way of spending the holidays even though my sons are now grown men.

Rosh Hashanah and Yom Kippur are holidays in which you can create your own form of worship and some of the books listed in the Appendix can serve as guides in this regard. You may choose to revere a Supreme Being or Life or simply the moment in time in which you find yourself. These sacred days are occasions that afford you an opportunity for renewal, rededication, and the recognition of responsibility to your fellow humans and other living creatures. And you can do all this fashioned in the manner of your people knowing that if you hallow the day in a way consistent with your heart, you do so as a Jew.

CHAPTER
27

Passover

Passover—or Pesach—has always been my favorite holiday, though for different reasons. As a child, I looked forward to the search for the Afikomen and receiving a reward for having retrieved it. Later, I basked in the spotlight of everyone's attention when chanting the Four Questions—an occasion when the youngster and not the adult took center stage. Before long came the opportunity to participate in the seder itself—reading from the Haggadah in Hebrew and English as the story of the escape from slavery to freedom unfolded before our very eyes. And later still, when the Seder was mine to conduct, I could arrange it to reflect my personal needs and outlook.

Throughout all this was the added constant which made Passover special. It was a family holiday. Not like other holidays spent in synagogue where, as a boy, I'd go off on my own to the youth services. No, on seder nights the family remained together. I remember my grandparents at our family seders and over the course of time, my parents and my wife's parents provided the generational linkage for my children along with aunts, uncles, and cousins. In fact, our seder table has always been open to anyone who wished to join us or who was otherwise alone on the holiday.

Yet all this said, I have not fully explained why Passover is so unique. You see, Pesach is more than a gathering of the clan and more than recounting the narrative of the Exodus. The light that illuminates the Seder night has this at the center of its flame: "Remember that you were a slave in the land of Egypt." And on four separate occasions in the Torah, we are commanded, "You shall tell your child" of the exodus from Egypt.

In these two simple yet heavily laden words, "remember" and "tell," is the gist of Passover and why it means so much to me. It makes no difference whether the edicts issued from God or Moses, or from priests and rabbis, or from the pen of a simple scrivener who thought it sounded good and had a nice ring. The force and the demand of the Passover commandments—remember and tell—is the heart and soul of being Jewish.

This is probably why on Passover I feel more compelled than ever to remember and tell of the Holocaust of which the Passover story is an ominous precursor. As Jonathan Kirsch points out in his book, *Moses: A Life*, Pharaoh's policy towards the Hebrew slaves was history's first recorded effort at genocide. Concerned about the burgeoning number of Hebrews, the Egyptians employed hard labor as a form of mass murder to cull the Hebrew population—a practice carried out even more methodically in the Nazi labor/death camps. Moreover, the slaughter of the firstborn Hebrew males was the first reported pogrom in history where the state sanctioned the entire citizenry to execute the edict.

But as horrific and singular as the Holocaust shall always remain, it is only part of the meaning of Passover. It is only one link—albeit an exceptional and burdensome one—in the chain that extends from the time we were slaves and left Egypt to stand at Sinai; to the stakes where we were bound with our flesh flayed by marauding crusaders; to when we were expelled from Spain or hid as Marranos; to the shtetls of Eastern Europe where we suffered the pogroms; and to the golden hills of Jerusalem when the Arab armies pounced on the tiny fledgling nation of Israel—again the world looking on with indifference.

Not in deference to these events, for in and of themselves they are nothing, but because of those Jews—our ancestors—people who lived and breathed—must we remember. Not for the sake of history, but for the sake of our children, grandchildren, and those yet to be born, must we tell. We must remember and we must tell. This is the essence of Passover. Which is why, as I said, Pesach is, has always been, and always will be, my favorite holiday.

Such are my feelings about Pesach. No Jewish holiday has a more universal appeal than the celebration of Passover. Not only does it tell the story of the Exodus and commemorate the time when the Hebrews embarked from slavery into freedom, but it heralds the day when freedom will come to people everywhere and no one need endure the yoke of oppression.

Every effort should be made each year at the Seder to relate the tale of the Exodus in such a manner as to relive its essence. As the Haggadah says: "Whoever enlarges upon the telling of the story of the Exodus from Egypt, that person is praiseworthy." Which is why you should not only feel free to add to the seder but consider it a responsibility. It is a singular opportunity when, in the name of tradition, you are free to be completely creative and augment the holiday in any fashion you wish!

This may be done in several ways. You can set aside some time to talk about passages in the haggadah you are using or discuss whatever is on someone's mind as you make your way through the seder. You also have the option to marshal material and read it as supplemental to the haggadah. Another alternative might be to write your very own family haggadah! It's not as difficult as it sounds.

In a contributing essay in *Zen and Hasidism*, Steve Sanfield wrote about developing his own Haggadah this way:

Passover became an important time for us, a time for renewal. We celebrated it with a seder that grew larger each year, using a Haggadah we put together ourselves. We took what was meaningful to us and left behind anything that didn't speak to us directly. We incorporated material from the American Indian, Chinese Buddhist, and Hasidic traditions and we included the songs and poems of our friends and contemporaries.

Now, you don't have to go so far afield unless, of course, you wish. In compiling my family haggadah, I took the approach of excerpting what was meaningful from a variety of haggadahs. As time went on, whenever I happened to be struck by what someone wrote about Pesach or appeared otherwise relevant, I added that as a supplement (with computers this becomes a very easy thing to do). The first edition of "The Bank Family Haggadah" was in 1987 and my younger son did the artwork. With numerous additions, it is now twice the size of the original though the artwork remains the same, much to my son's chagrin.

There is a wealth of material you may consider either as supplemental readings or to begin the process of composing your own haggadah. Please feel free to peruse and consider what follows in this regard. In addition, there is a list of haggadahs ranging from the traditional to the more contemporary to even what may be called "avant-garde."

> *Stripped of all the natural and historical impossibilities, the story tells us that a people, languishing for generations in slavery, found the courage to break out of its yoke, wander in a desert wilderness, suffer hunger and thirst . . . face death and despair, but in the end, inspired by a compelling progressive ideal, attained its goal and entered the Promised Land. What do all these divine miracles mean against that one simple, human, shiningly-beautiful fact? All of humanity would do well to celebrate the Jewish Passover.*
> *—Chaim Zhitlovsky*

> *"The Seder of 'The Simple'"*
> *   Then my wife woke me, and it was evening, and she said to me: "Why don't you celebrate the Seder like all other Jews?" Said I: "What do you want with me? I am an ignorant man, and my father was an ignorant man, and I don't know what to do and what not to do. But one thing I know: Our fathers and mothers were in captivity in the land of the Gypsies, and we have a God, and He led them out, and into freedom. And see: now we are again in captivity and I know and I tell you that God will lead us to freedom too."*
> *   And then I saw before me a table, and the cloth gleamed like the sun, and on it were platters with matzot and eggs and other dishes, and bottles of red wine. I ate of the matzot and eggs and drank of the wine, and gave my wife to eat and to-drink. And then I was overcome with joy, and lifted my cup to God, and said: "See,*

*God, I drink this cup to You! And do You lean down and make us
free!''*

—Hasidic Tale

*Like the khoomitz Pop used to brush up with a feather the morning
before the first Passover night, crumbs of unleavened bread. Went
into a wooden spoon. Tied up with a rag. And burned in the
streets. . . . Hey Mickey, hey Feeney, hey Maloney, you know
what this is? It's khoomitz, a few dry bread crumbs. So they'll say,
Yeah? Waddaye do wit' it? And you'll say, Burn it in the street. And
they'll say, Go ahead, we'll piss on it. You Jews are nuts. . . .*

*Passover. Pesach. Matzahs. When Moses led the Hebrews
out of bondage. Talk about bondage. Boy, he could yell, Nates,
nates, nates! He knew the fancy name, as he did so many others.
Natey, nickname for a Jewboy. But to be understood, he'd have to
yell like a wop. . . . And that was before Passover. Moses—or
was it God?—parted the Red Sea with a titanic—nah, cosmic
command. How the hell could one little Israelite guy with one little
staff split a whole sea asunder, cause such a cataclysm?*

—Henry Roth

*The seder has a potent appeal even for an irreligious Jew like me,
not least of all because its ceremonial belongs not to the synagogue but to the home. The dialogue is between parent and child
rather than between rabbi and congregation. Like no other Jewish
festival, it combines homeliness with holiness.*

—Theo Richmond

*Jews should, therefore, celebrate the festival of Pesach as a stimu-
lus not merely to effect Jewish self-emancipation, but also to further
universal self-emancipation from all forms of bondage whereby
man suppresses the personality and individuality of his fellow.*

—Mordecai Kaplan

*Faceless animal suffering is to the modern industrial world what
the faceless serf was to feudalism or the faceless slave to a slave
economy. Faceless suffering is an abomination . . . and the Haggadah is the right place to say that.*

*Among the intuited visions in prophetic writing is the need for
reconciliation between natural man and historical man to heal the*

human condition. The practice of vegetarianism is a good place to begin this process of healing. Merely by ceasing to eat meat, merely by practicing restraint, we have the power to end a painful industry. Most often, the act of repairing the world, of healing moral wounds, is left to heroes and tzaddikim, saints and people of unusual discipline. But here is an action every mortal can perform.

All life is sacred. Let us live in this wisdom: to heal and not to harm, to revere and to sanctify, to bless and not abuse, to choose life. . . .

—Haggadah for the Liberated Lamb

At most Passover celebrations, participants make a Hillel sandwich. . . . While the sharpness of the horseradish brings stinging tears to the eyes, the tongue tastes intense sweetness. The vexed relationship between Judaism and feminism seems to me that the pleasure I and many of my contemporaries can receive from our heritage will always be mixed with sorrow, the pride with grief, the joy with anger, sweetness and bitterness, honey on the tongue with tears in the eyes.

—Susan Gubar

Tonight would be the beginning of Passover. It was the time for my encounter with the sacred past. . . . A time to recite in high and solemn tones the archaic English of my old Haggadah. A time to leave the turmoil of America, of 1968, of burning streets, and napalmed villages. . . . A time for ceremonious pleasure.

But not this afternoon. As I walked up Eighteenth Street toward my house, my steps began to drum an eerie sentence: "This is Pharaoh's Army . . . And I am on my way to do Seder." And when I turned the corner at Wyoming Avenue, there it was still: a United States Army jeep, machine gun pointing vaguely at my house. The rhythmic chant came back again, this time a question: "This is Pharaoh's chariot . . . And I am on my way to do the Seder?"

That night, for the first time, I broke open the form of the Haggadah to talk about the streets and what had happened to us. For the first time I felt the Seder a moment not for high and solemn recitation, but for burning and hard thinking. For the first time, we paused to talk about its meaning.

—Arthur Waskow

In April 1943, on the first day of Passover, a nucleus of Jews immured in the Ghetto declared war on powerful Germany, rose up in arms, incredibly won the first battle, and finally were exterminated.

In the mosaic of European resistance, the struggle of the Warsaw Ghetto occupies a unique place. Those insurgents had no rear lines at their back, they did not expect help from land or sky, they had no allies; on the contrary, for years they had been living under the most wretched conditions.

At a distance of forty years and in an ever more restless world, we do not want the sacrifice of the Warsaw Ghetto insurgents to be forgotten. They have demonstrated that even when everything is lost, it is granted to man to save, together with his own dignity, that of future generations.

—Primo Levi

How could I not love Passover? For weeks we lived in a state of anticipation filled with endless preparations. Passover meant the end of winter, the victory of spring, the triumph of childhood.

I still follow the rituals, of course. But in the deepest part of myself, I know it's not the same. An abyss separates me from the child I once was. Today I know no happiness can be complete. Do I love it less than before? Let's just say I love it differently.

What significance does Passover have, if not to keep the memories alive? To be Jewish is to take up the burden of the past and include it in our concerns, our projects, and our obligations in the present.

Although man has conquered space . . . wars continue to rage, victims fall to terrorists' bullets, children die of hunger and disease . . . why is there so much hatred in the world? And why so much indifference to suffering, to the anguish of others?

I love Passover because it remains for me a cry against insensitivity.

—Elie Wiesel

HAGGADAHS TO CONSIDER

A variety of haggadahs and books about Passover are available— especially as the holiday approaches when you can usually find a diverse selection at regular bookstores. In addition, you can peruse stores that carry Judaica and synagogue shops. Look through periodicals where they may be advertised. For example, in vegetarian magazines you will find information on obtaining "The Haggadah for the Liberated Lamb," or in women's periodicals like *Lilith*, an haggadah with a feminist bent.

A sampling is listed below and where possible, the full address of the publisher is provided as you can always obtain copies from them. By the way, if you are buying more than a few haggadahs from the publisher directly, don't forget to ask for a discount!

Every Person's Guide to Passover. Ronald Isaac. Jason Aronson Inc., 230 Livingston Street, Northvale NJ, 201-767-4093. More of a guide, this book offers an overview of the history, traditions, and rituals associated with the holiday and advice on how to prepare for the seder. Obtainable in bookstores or from the publisher.

A Passover Haggadah. The New Union Haggadah prepared by the Central Conference of American Rabbis. Edited by Herbert Bronstein. Traditional haggadah but user–friendly with some contemporary additions. Available in many bookstores.

The Passover Haggadah. General Israel Orphan's Home For Girls in Jerusalem. This traditional haggadah contains artwork of the children and can be obtained from the New York office: 132 Nassau Street, New York, NY 10038.

The New Model Seder. Edited by Rabbi Sidney Greenberg and S. Allan Sugarman. The Prayer Book Press of Media Judaica, Inc., 1363 Fairfield Ave., Bridgeport, CT, 06605. Contemporary material combined with much of the contents of the standard haggadah makes for a seder with something for just about everyone and its conciseness promises dinner at a reasonable hour!

Family Passover Haggadah. Published by the Union of Orthodox Jewish Congregations. Though traditional, this haggadah, with illustrations by Dreamworks, has a universal appeal. It includes questions and clues to hold the attention of those at the seder. Look for its web site: www.familyhaggadah.com.

Haggadah for a Secular Celebration of Pesach. Sholom Aleichem Club of Philadelphia, 463 E. Wadsworth Ave., Philadelphia, PA 19119. Available from the publisher or in some bookstores. For starters, it opens left to right and that says it all! A recounting of the story of the Exodus, without the miracles and the supernatural, emphasizing the cultural, historical, sociological, and philosophical importance of the event.

Artscroll Youth Haggadah. Published by Mesorah, includes illustrations and interesting commentary.

The Santa Cruz Haggadah. Karen G.R. Roekard. The Hineni Consciousness Press. Berkeley, CA. 510-843-4952. www.santacruz hag.com. "A Passover Haggadah, coloring book and journal for the evolving consciousness." [New Age Judaism]

The Illuminated Haggadah. Stewart, Taborit & Chang, Publishers. A concise/traditional beautifully illustrated haggadah with pictorials from the Haggadah Collection of the British Museum.

Passover Haggadah. New Revised Edition. Rabbi Nathan Goldberg. Ktav Publishing House, Inc. Hoboken, NJ, 07030. A traditional haggadah.

The New American Haggadah. Developed by Mordecai Kaplan, Ira Eisenstein, and Eugene Kohn. Edited by Gila Gevirtz. Behrman House, Inc. A fairly traditional, but Reconstructionist, haggadah designed to reflect contemporary tastes and concerns.

A Passover Haggadah. With commentary by Elie Wiesel and illustrations by Mark Podwal. Simon & Schuster.

The Family Seder. Rabbi Alfred J. Kolatch. Jonathan David Publishers, Inc. A traditional haggadah. Also available from this publisher is an abridged version—*The Concise Family Seder.*

Why On This Night? A Passover Haggadah for Family Celebration. Rahel Musleah, illustrated by Louise August. Simon & Schuster. A children's haggadah.

A Survivors' Haggadah. Jewish Publication Society. (800-234-3151). Originally composed and used by Holocaust survivors in a displaced persons' camp on the first Passover after Liberation.

CHAPTER
28

Chanukah

Our history is replete with "firsts." As we saw in the last chapter, the slaying of the firstborn Hebrew males by the Egyptians marked the first recorded instance of genocide. The Hebrews were the first people to bring monotheism to the world. And Chanukah marks yet another "first"—the first rebellion for religious freedom.

Freedom is the keystone of the Jewish value system. Without it, we are unable to pursue anything else. As nomads, the early Hebrews were free to live their lives in accordance with their newly adopted covenant with God and monotheism. Escaping Egypt and slavery, the Jews were free once again to conduct themselves consistent with their beliefs. Over the millennia and particularly during the Diaspora, our freedom has often been curtailed but always resolutely fought for.

Chanukah celebrates the successful victory in pursuit of religious liberty. But there is another aspect to the Chanukah story which has been little noted and bears mention. I came upon it recently and wrote about it for a Jewish publication, *Inside Magazine*. I'd like to share it with you now.

ANOTHER CHANUKAH

Fond memories of Hebrew school are few and far between but one that stands out has to do with the celebration of Chanukah. I was nine or ten when my class staged a play about the holiday and, while I did not get the leading role of the heroic Judah Maccabee, who bravely engaged the Syrians in battle after battle ultimately returning in triumph to the temple in Jerusalem, I was assigned the part of his father Mattathias, the priest who started it all.

I was very tall for my age and I towered over my fellow thespians as I strode to center stage at the play's beginning. Sneering at the officer attempting to enforce Antiochus's decree that Jews must comply with idolatrous worship, I boldly proclaimed: "I and my sons and brethren walk in the covenant of our fathers. Heaven forbid that we should forsake the Law!" Then, I raised my arm and forcefully struck the soldier and shouted, "Let everyone who is zealous for the Law . . . follow me!"

My chest puffed and I preened like a peacock as I strutted across the stage. The audience was transfixed—indeed, inspired. Such was our enactment of the first rebellion for religious liberty. But there is another aspect to the saga of Chanukah that either I never knew or else might have forgotten because it was treated with insignificance. Yet, it is becoming increasingly relevant today and should be recounted more prominently.

The part of the Chanukah story I did not act out is this. It seems that in the burning eyes of Mattathias Maccabee, even more repugnant than the Syrian soldiers were the Hellenized Jews. The old priest's "zeal was kindled" and when one such Jew came forward to comply with the decrees, Mattathias killed him even before he slew the soldier, for so much more vile was the apostate.

I don't think I would have been thrilled to have had to perform the scene of murdering a fellow Jew and I'm not sure how it would have sat with the audience, which is why it was probably cut from the script. I do know that I am troubled by this now but not so much that it took place—for this was centuries ago and Mattathias was a man of his time and culture. Rather, I am disturbed by what this narrative from our history, so pertinent today, may portend for our future if we do not heed its lessons.

We are wrong to think that the question of Jewish identity is a new dilemma. Indeed, it is presumptuous of us. Clearly, the matter of "Who is a Jew?" was very much in the forefront of Mattathias Maccabee's mind when he killed his assimilated "brother." Greater than the danger posed by the Syrian oppressors was the threat from within—from those Jews Mattathias deemed not to be "Jewish" enough. And what is the appropriate punishment for assimilation? Why death, of course.

Perhaps what we should remember most about Chanukah is not the successful rebellion nor the miracle of the lights but rather the killing of one Jew by another for the simple reason, in the eyes of the murderer, that it was a justifiable—even laudable deed. In the pursuit of preserving one's system of belief, a human life pales in comparison. The ends justify the means. It is the soil from which future assassins of Israeli prime ministers germinate.

Cries of derision and shoving and throwing stones by haredim against Reform Jews and women at the Western Wall of the very same temple liberated by Judah Maccabee are only a step removed from the example set by Mattathias. Likewise, hatred and acts of provocation shown by secular Jews toward their religious counterparts only exacerbate the malignancy.

There is a reason the Bible portrays our ancestors as very human. Moses speaking God's message with a stutter; David dispatching his lover's husband to his death; Joseph's brothers selling him into slavery and so on. We should learn the lessons of our fallible progenitors—emulate their worthy actions and avoid their mistakes. So it should be with Chanukah and for the moment, the greatest lesson lies in what not to do.

By and large, Jews in the Diaspora are fortunate to live in freedom. Moreover, for the first time in 2000 years, we have a Jewish homeland. At least for the present, the need to follow the ways of Judah Maccabee is not necessary. But we all would do well to repudiate the action taken by his father and instead come together as one people with a shared history and tradition and system of belief. We should take pride in our coat of many colors containing a myriad of fabrics that, when woven together, make us what we are.

If only I could go back to that stage at my Hebrew school, what literary license I would exercise! I would make the episode involving the Hellenized Jew the focus of the play but with a twist. I, as Mattathias

Maccabee, would not slay my fellow Jew, nor would I even wield a fist in anger or raise my voice above speaking tone. No. Instead, I'd embrace the man and engage in a dialogue recognizing that what we Jews have in common far surpasses our differences. It is not the prerogative of any Jew or rabbinical court or political party to disenfranchise another Jew. And for that matter, it is not the right of anyone to ostracize any person or group from the greater community of humans. We Jews know where this leads having been maligned by the Nazi doctrine and transformed into something not human.

Which is why, this year, it is the story of the other Chanukah which I will share when we light the candles on the menorah and chant the melody we have been singing for hundreds of years. For once I will not dwell on the heroism of Judah but instead, I will focus my attention on the crime committed by his father and do my best to avoid a similar fate.

Just as I saw Chanukah in another light (no pun intended since Chanukah is the "Feast of Lights"), as with every holiday, you should feel free to interpret it as you wish and imbue it with what is meaningful and important to you. And like Passover, though there are special prayer services for Chanukah, this is a festival primarily celebrated in the home so once again, you are at liberty to have your home reflect the way you want to observe the event.

Naturally there are the traditional observances: the lighting of the menorah and chanting the blessings; singing Chanukah songs; spinning the dreidel; and the giving of Chanukah gelt and gifts. And speaking of gifts, how about gathering some old clothes or foodstuffs and, with your family, distributing these to the homeless or people in need? What better way to promote the spirit of the holiday and set an example for your children!

I suppose the thing we all strive to avoid is the comparison with Christmas and the idea Chanukah is merely a Jewish substitute. Take pride in things Jewish and Chanukah should be no exception. Even the dubious action of Mattathias Maccabee does not diminish the courage our Jewish forebears exhibited in battling for religious liberty and freedom. Be proud in being a Jew, share this with your loved ones, and celebrate Chanukah and all our holidays in a sincere and meaningful way.

CHAPTER
29

The Sabbath

Remember the sabbath day, to keep it holy. Six days shalt thou labour, and do all thy work; but the seventh day is a sabbath unto the Lord thy God, in it thou shalt not do any manner of work, thou, nor thy son, nor thy daughter, nor thy man-servant, nor thy maid-servant, nor thy cattle, nor thy stranger that is within thy gates; for in six days the Lord made heaven and earth, the sea, and all that in them is, and rested on the seventh day; wherefore the Lord blessed the sabbath day, and hallowed it.

—*Exodus 20:8-11*

The Fifth of the Ten Commandments singles out the Sabbath as a holy day. It is, of course, the only holiday mentioned in the Decalogue and for that reason, it is the most sacred day of the year during which it occurs no less than fifty-two times! What an opportunity!

Over the course of our history, this is precisely what Jews have done—honored the Sabbath and kept it holy. Which is not to say there have been, and indeed still remain, different ways to go about this even though the "shalts" and "shalt nots" are rather well defined. According to *halakhah*, the proscriptions of the Sabbath are delineated to the minutiae and to some—like a rambunctious 8-year-old on summer vacation—it makes for a stifling time giving rise to resentment. Allow me to explain.

Though Conservative, my mother's parents were very observant and as a result, when they joined us for summer holiday in the Catskills, we had to select a strictly kosher establishment. A small hotel was chosen and since most of the guests were Orthodox, the hotelier made certain the environs passed muster. Thus, it came to pass that I spent my first Sabbath under the dictates of *halakha*.

I awoke in the morning and bustled down the stairs to discover the television draped with a white sheet. Breakfast was cold cereal although there was hot chocolate because the burner was left on from before sundown on Friday. A gorgeous day for a swim but the pool gate was locked. Men were in the corner davening making so much noise I just had to get out.

The badminton racquets were *verboten* as was ball playing and even running games. A friend I had made joined me in opting to escape from the "prison" in which we found ourselves. We roamed about a hundred yards beyond the main house when we came upon a rope stretched out before us demarcating the limits of permissible distance which could be traversed on the Sabbath. Glancing guilty looks between us, my friend and I slipped under the rope and ran as fast as we could, gleefully shouting and bounding in the air, thrilled to be free of the constraints of the day.

I haven't changed much regarding my opinion of such things and I still marvel at the way the Sabbath is observed by the Orthodox. Sometimes, it proves a battleground among us Jews. In Israel, haredim throw rocks at secular Jews driving cars in their neighborhood or going to a movie. In Miami Beach at the condominium where my parents have a residence, the biggest bone of contention is whether to designate the service elevator as a "Shabbes" elevator. And by the way, it's not Gentile versus Jew; but Jew versus Jew.

All this aside, I respect the Orthodox for the way they have chosen to abide by the Fifth Commandment. In fact, the Orthodox have set a worthy example for us all in contending for the right to observe the Sabbath. Consider what Sholem Asch had written of an effort to achieve better working conditions during the early part of the twentieth century:

After two weeks of a bitter strike in which the pious Jews displayed a marked ability to fight, they returned to the shop with "timbrels and dancing." They had won all their demands. And the first demand was: "that the Sabbath will be observed and time for mincha will be allowed. Along with this went a raise in pay, and union hours."

But for you and me, I think we can put the Sabbath into another perspective which is something many Jews, religious and secular, have started to do. The purpose of the Sabbath is to establish one day of the week during which we set aside the mundane matters that occupy our hectic lives. How you fill it is really up to you.

In an essay written for the *Forward*, Nan Chase, a writer, relates her transition from being a person with vague Jewish roots to being a Jew in more than name only. She and her husband accomplished this by observing the Sabbath "while adapting the practices to our tastes, temperaments, and times." The result was a home imbued with Jewish values and discussions with their children who, as a result, developed a keen interest in things Jewish.

The same opportunity awaits you. Make the Sabbath a time when you and your family are together. Really talk to each other about things of consequence. Have a Friday night dinner—with or without the candle lighting or blessings over the wine and bread. Attend a Sabbath service or *havurah* if you are so inclined. Take time by yourself to read or write. Go for a serene walk in the woods or park. Contemplate the world around you. Observe what's going on out there and within yourself. Take some quiet time.

No one, least of all me, can tell you what to do on the Sabbath. Or, for that matter, what not to do. Remember, my idea in being Jewish means you make the decisions. Employ the traditional rituals and practices of the Sabbath you desire and, if you want, modify them to suit your needs. Feel free to add whatever it is to make the time meaningful—regardless of how "untraditional" that may be.

Must you do this *every* Sabbath for the *entire* period from sundown to sundown? I think not. Nor should you feel guilty or any less Jewish if you miss some Sabbath days or even decide it's not on your agenda at all. But at the same time, there is a lot to be said for having fifty-two days each year to set aside and make special. The important thing is to seize the day, and fill it with activities which are meaningful.

The Sabbath is one more thing the Jews have contributed to the world. And in hallowing the Sabbath, take pride that you do it as a Jew.

PART VII

Jewish Organizations One or More for You!

CHAPTER
30

Zionists and Supporters of Israel

TRAIN TO NOWHERE

Sometime on 9 November 1938, under the cover of night, my grand-parents boarded a train bound for nowhere. Or, more precisely, the train pulling out of an otherwise empty station in the German town of Odenbach did have a destination. It's just that my grandparents did not.

While the house where they had lived and raised a family was being ransacked by SA troopers, assorted Nazi thugs, and anti-semitic rabble, my grandparents slipped away unnoticed. With few worldly possessions, they stole down the street, glancing back only once to see a neighbor rummage through the clothing piled on the curb. My grandparents never saw their home again.

Until this time, Hitler's plan for Germany to become "judenrein" was to make life so unbearable for the Jews that they would emigrate. However, there were a number of factors working against this, includ-ing the aged population of German Jews, the belief that Hitler was just another anti-semitic storm that would ultimately pass, the limited quo-tas set by countries on the Jews they would allow in, and Arab pressure on England engendering severe restrictions on Jewish immigration to Palestine. As a result, by 1938, only one third of the 525,000 Jews living in Germany when Hitler came to power had relocated elsewhere and, for the Third Reich, this was simply not enough.

Using as an excuse the killing of a legation secretary in the German embassy in Paris by a Polish Jew named Herschel Grynszpan, the Third Reich unleashed the virulent throngs and added a new dimension to the persecution of Germany's Jews. When Kristallnacht, as the bleak hours of November 9th and 10th came to be known, reached a fiery end, Hitler had instigated the worst pogrom in German history: 500 synagogues were burned; seven thousand Jewish businesses were destroyed; tens of thousands of homes were invaded; ninety Jews were killed; hundreds of women were raped; and thirty thousand Jews were arrested.

Shortly thereafter, an article appeared in an SS publication that signaled that the "final solution of the Jewish question" would be exclusion from the economy, confiscation of any remaining wealth, enclosure into a ghetto, and destruction by "fire and the sword." Plunder, starvation, and death became the only prospects for Jews inside the Third Reich.

In the ten months following Kristallnacht, another 100,000 to 150,000 Jews fled the country that had been their home for centuries. Those who stayed behind did so for one reason only—they had nowhere to go; which is what made my grandparents' frantic hours endured on a lurching train both symbolic and prophetic.

A sympathetic conductor, who knew my grandfather from his frequent business trips, cautioned them not to disembark in Mainz where they had family. It was much too dangerous, he whispered. They had no money to go any farther, but he allowed them to remain until late the next day when they scurried off in the city of Furth skulking through alleyways to a temporary haven with other family members.

Like all German Jews after Kristallnacht, my grandparents were without assets, dispossessed of their home, and in fear of their lives. The Nazis created the greatest "catch-22" of all time. In order to avoid death, the Jews must leave—"Raus Juden!"—but in order to emigrate, they had to have the funds to pay the exorbitant exit fees and be able to demonstrate to the country of their destination that they had capital and would not be a burden. Much as the German government wanted the Jews gone, they made it practically impossible for them to comply.

Only two weeks earlier, my grandparents had managed to dis-

patch their two daughters to the United States, not knowing if they would see them again. After Kristallnacht, they held even less hope of reaching America. Instead, my grandparents felt the way they did during those interminable hours spent on a train rambling through the night. But this time there was not even the promise of dawn, and the next train that would come for them would have a destination beyond their most horrific nightmare. Somehow, it was a train they managed to avoid.

As survivors' stories go, my grandparents fared rather well, having eluded the killing camps. Yet, Theresienstadt, where they were interned for three years, was no "show case," as Hitler would have had the world believe. It became a way station for Auschwitz, and of the 30,000 liberated at war's end, only 4,000 survived the ravages of disease. Of the 164,000 Jews who did not leave Germany, more than three-quarters were murdered in the Shoah.

My grandparents never spoke to me of this time in their lives—partly, because they never learned English, and my German was elementary. But the more fundamental reason is that, like many survivors, it was something they did not wish to discuss. When I did finally grasp the enormity of the Shoah, it was from Holocaust literature seen through the eyes of Elie Wiesel, Viktor Frankl, and Primo Levi. Compared to Buchenwald, Treblinka, and Auschwitz, Theresienstadt and Kristallnacht paled by comparison. Of what importance could they hold for me?

This was a mistake. In its own way, Kristallnacht is portentous even today, for its evil was insidious—slinking up almost from nowhere, stalking its unsuspecting victims and slowly encircling them with its lethal tentacles, wringing the very life out of them. And when it did manifest its face, it was too late.

I believe that each survivor has a unique message. When I try to discern what my grandparents' experience has to offer, I eventually realize that their message is not to be found in the confines of Theresienstadt or in the preceding years when they were transformed from respected German citizens of Jewish faith to demonic creatures not even human. What they have to say has to do with those hours spent on a train to nowhere.

Oddly enough, this was conveyed to me in another way when I was six or seven. My father's mother, who came to America from Russia when she was in her teens, used to sing me a song in Yiddish and then in English. Its words and melody haunt me to this day. I can hear its tune in perfect harmony with the clanging of a train on the railroad tracks while my mind's eye envisions a Jewish couple hunched in the shadows, jostling to and fro, their hands clasped together as they stare into the bleakness of the passing night.

Like the repeated rasping of the metal wheels against steel, I hear my father's mother intone over and over, "Wie ahin zul ich gayn? Wie ahin zul ich gayn?" I realize now that the way she gazed down at me must have been how my grandparents looked when they peered out of the train windows on the "night of the broken glass."

"Where shall I go? Where shall I go?" My head throbs as the question resonates along the rails, again and again, demanding an answer.

Where to go when there is nowhere to go? This was the question I imagined gnawing at my grandparents that infamous night and which prompted me to write *Train To Nowhere*, first published in *Midstream*. The answer came in 1948 when, like the mythical phoenix, the modern State of Israel arose from the ashes of the Holocaust.

No doubt, uppermost in the minds of Jews living in the Shoah's shadow was to establish a safe haven for Jews the world over. Today, this remains a potent reason to support the Jewish homeland—not out of paranoia but because, if not in the United States, there are places all across the globe where it is precarious to be Jewish. Moreover, given our history of two thousand years in Diaspora, there is no reason to believe this will change anytime soon.

Perhaps this rings true to you and makes you want to become an advocate for Israel. But there are other compelling reasons to support the Jewish state you might want to contemplate. Consider what Israel's first president and first prime minister had to say:

It is our people who once gave the world a spiritual message fundamental to civilization. The world is watching us now to see the way we choose in ordering our lives, how we fashion our State. The world is listening to hear whether a new message will go forth from Zion, and what that message will be.

—Chaim Weizmann

We have always been a small people numerically and we shall remain a small people, unable to compete with our rivals in population, territory, natural resources and strengths of armed forces. But the place of our country in the world cannot be measured in quantitative terms. Few people have had so profound an influence upon so large a part of the human race. And there are few countries which have played so central a role in world history as the Land of Israel.

—David Ben-Gurion

Israel can be a beacon to the world holding itself to a higher standard than the banner of nationalism implies for other countries. But no one else has the right to impose this burden upon the State of Israel, although we Jews can take it up of our own accord.

To fortify your ties with Israel, you might want to think about a visit. I remember how my bubbe who sang to me, *Wie ahin zul ich gayn*, always spoke with a faraway gleam in her eyes about one day going there. But it was not to be. Years later, when I stepped off the plane and for the first time set my feet on Jewish soil, I could not help but think of her and all my forebears who clung to the unrealized dream of standing in the Promised Land. I could feel the yearnings of centuries coarse through my arteries and, though I've been back since, that was the moment which will always stand out.

There are many ways you can arrange to visit Israel and numerous itineraries available. You can do so through a Jewish organization or synagogue or any travel agent. I am sure you've heard about bar and bat mitzvahs in Israel but whether or not you use that as an occasion to make the journey, bringing your children with you or sending them on their own under the auspices of one of many educational programs or organized groups will certainly have a profound effect upon them. If your children have not been exposed to a formal Jewish education or are rejecting Judaism—the religion, this is an excellent way to expose them to another side of being Jewish.

Because what they'll see is a country where half the Jews have nothing whatsoever to do with religion and regard themselves as secular. But these Jews have no doubt about being Jews, nor should they. By involving yourself in some way with Israel, no matter how small, you will have discovered a fulfilling means to reinforce your Jewish identity.

Of course, while you have the option of making aliyah, you can remain in the United States and still be involved in activities supporting Israel. There are many organizations covering the spectrum from political support to providing social and health services to contributing funds for education, scientific endeavors, and religious purposes.

Here are some of the organizations you may want to consider if this is a path you wish to explore. The information provided indicates the national office although there may be a local office or chapter near you.

Abraham Fund. 477 Madison Ave. New York, NY 10022. Supports coexistence between Israeli Arabs & Jews.

American Associates, Ben-Gurion University of the Negev. 342 Madison Ave., Suite 1224, New York, NY 10173, (212) 687-7721. Provides financial support and raises awareness for the university which concentrates on development of the Negev region.

American Committee for Shaare Zedek Hospital in Jerusalem, Inc. 49 W. 45th Street, Suite 1100, New York, NY 10036, (212) 354-8801. Publicizes and raises funds for this hospital which serves all Israeli citizens.

American Committee for the Weizmann Institute of Science. 51 Madison Ave., New York, NY 10010, (212) 779-2500. Supports this scientific institute and graduate school which focuses on combating disease and hunger as well as protecting the environment and developing new sources of energy.

American Friends of Bar-Ilan University. New York. (212) 673-3460.

American Friends of Hebrew University. 11 E. 69th St., New York, NY 10021, (212) 472-9800.

American Technion Society. 810 7th Ave., 24th Floor, New York, NY 10019, (212) 262-6200. Supports the Israel Institute of Technology.

Americans For Peace Now. 1835 K. Street, NW, Suite 500, Washington, DC 20006, (202) 728-1893. Assists the Peace Now Organization in Israel.

Amit-Women. 817 Broadway, New York, NY 10003, (212) 477-

4720. Raises funds for social welfare, youth programs, and other projects in Israel.

Boys Town Jerusalem, Foundation of America. 12 W. 31st Street, Suite 300, New York, NY 10001, (212) 244-2766. Aids this educational center for disadvantaged students with academic, technical, and Torah programs.

General Israel Orphans' Home for Girls/Jerusalem. 132 Nassau Street, New York, NY 10038, (212) 267-7222.

Jewish National Fund. (800) 542-8733. Undertakes conservation and reclamation projects in Israel as well as planting trees.

Maccabi USA/Sports for Israel. 1926 Arch Street, Philadelphia, PA 19103, (215) 561-6900. Promotes sports and athletic facilities in Israel and U.S. participation in the Maccabiah Games.

New Israel Fund. 111 W. 40th Street, Suite 2300, New York, NY 10010. Helps organizations in Israel which promote social equality, civil rights, and other progressive causes.

The **American Zionist Movement** (AZM), is an umbrella organization for a number of Zionist groups. You can obtain information regarding its member organizations by contacting their office: 110 East 59th Street, New York, NY 10022, (212) 318-6100.

Several of the member groups of AZM are:

Na'amat USA. Provides training, special services, and education for women and youth in Israel.

Hadassah—Women's Zionist Organization of America. 50 W. 58th Street, New York, NY 10019, (888) 303-3640. Conducts programs for teaching, research, and medicine in Israel and promotes Israel to the American public.

Zionist Organization of America. 4 East 34th Street, New York, NY 10016, (212) 481-1500. Works for the security and welfare of Israel conducting campaigns to garner government and public support for economic and military aid.

The remaining member groups of AZM, excluding affiliate organizations, are: American Friends of Meretz / American Jewish League for Israel / American Zionist Youth Council / Association of Reform Zionists of America / Bnai Zion / Emunah of America / Friends of Likud / Labor Zionist Alliance / Mercaz-Zionist Organization of

Conservative Judaism / Religious Zionists of America / Zionist Student Movement.

What a list! And there are even more.

That's the thing about us Jews. So few of us but so many options and each with its own agenda and mission. You know, it's like the story about the two Jews who moved to a small town in the Midwest. After trying to agree on starting a congregation, they wound up with three synagogues!

Which brings us to our next chapter—synagogues. And that makes a Chinese menu boring!

CHAPTER
31

Synagogues—
More Branches than a Tree!

Remember in Chapter 1 when I said you're not alone if you're a Jew who is not affiliated with any Jewish organization or synagogue? And how I emphasized that millions of Jews, perhaps even a majority, are not religious and either have nothing to do with prayer services or just as soon wish they hadn't? Well, the thing is that this isn't something which suddenly surfaced out of nowhere and is unique to the American Jewish community as we've turned a new millennium. It's been going on for quite a long time. In fact, I would venture to say that as long as there have been temples, synagogues, and houses of worship, there have been Jews who absented themselves or attended reluctantly.

But what is new is that in the last half of the twentieth century, many synagogues came to accept this state of affairs and have acclimated themselves by having features which have nothing whatsoever to do with prayer. In fact, you are likely to discover a variety of secular activities offered by most congregations.

First and foremost, a great amount of attention is paid to children. Some synagogues provide preschool programs. Formal Hebrew school education is available through bar and bat mitzvah and generally confirmation. Most synagogues have youth groups and we'll look into this in more detail in Chapter 42.

Adult education may take the form of courses or one-night programs with guest speakers. Discussion groups and study groups are often held. We will explore this further in Chapter 40. On the social side, there are the Men's Clubs and Sisterhoods although they may go by another name. For the seniors, programs and field trips frequently take place.

In other words, there is something for just about everyone and you can avail yourself of whatever you choose. And while there may be a Jewish community center near you, a synagogue is another option in fortifying your Jewish identity.

Of course, as opposed to a Jewish community center, synagogues include a religious component. These are, after all, houses of worship and if it's prayer you want—be it three days a year, every Sabbath, or daily minyan—this is where you get it. But even if you have no intention of ever setting foot inside the sanctuary, you still may want to associate yourself with a specific type of synagogue where you would feel more comfortable. Here you face a myriad of choices because, as I said in this Chapter's title, there are more branches than on a tree.

This is a fairly recent phenomenon. When I went to Hebrew school, there were three kinds of synagogues—Orthodox, Conservative, and Reform. Now as I look about me, I see a veritable Jacob's coat of many colors!

At one end of the spectrum, we have the Orthodox but even this has its subdivisions. There's the "Orthodox," the "modern Orthodox," the "Sephardic Orthodox," the "traditional Orthodox," and recently a hybrid of Orthodox and Conservative—the "Conserva-dox."

Naturally, there are the Conservative and Reform congregations most of which belong to their respective national federations. On the whole, there appears to be a trend within these respective denominations toward the traditional. For example, some Reform synagogues are looking more Conservative with men donning yarmulkes and talaysim, some of the women covering their heads, and more Hebrew in the service. In 1999, the Reform movement adopted new guidelines promoting greater observance of *halakhah*.

Meanwhile in the middle ground (if there is such a thing), an increased number of Conservative congregations are resembling the Orthodox by encouraging their members to "keep kosher" and strictly observe the Sabbath.

Where in all this does the Reconstructionist movement fit? This can be difficult to ascertain. Their innovations and willingness to adapt to current conditions, such as the ordination of women and gays and the acceptance of non-Jewish spouses, place these synagogues at the liberal end of the scale but many practices ring almost of orthodoxy. And again, some Reconstructionist congregations do not belong to the umbrella organization so they pretty much do as they like.

As if there weren't enough limbs on the Jewish tree from which to choose, a number of congregations call themselves "Independent," with each having its own set of conventions. Several of these Independent synagogues adhere to the Jewish Renewal movement.

There are even "meditation synagogues" which employ meditation techniques in the Jewish prayer service. Though mostly on the West Coast, these synagogues are scattered across the country. Two such congregations are: Bet Aleph Meditation Synagogue, Seattle, WA, (206) 527-9399, and Makam Ohr Shalom, Northridge, CA, (818) 725-7600.

I would be remiss if I did not mention minyanim and havurot, small prayer and study groups. The emphasis is on informality and intimacy. In addition to the obvious, some social activity is occasionally included.

There are many ways to go about selecting a synagogue. You can call the congregations which are geographically acceptable and gather information directly from each. Chances are, you will find them most receptive because membership is always a priority. This will also allow you to reach Independent and unaffiliated congregations.

Another option, especially if you know you want to belong to a particular denomination, is to contact the respective national umbrella organization and obtain the names of their constituent synagogues in your locale. These organizations are:

Union of American Hebrew Congregations (Reform), 633 Third Ave., New York, NY 10017, (212) 650-4000.

United Synagogue of Conservative Judaism, 8080 Old York Rd., Suite 209, Elkins Park, PA 19027, (215) 635-9701.

Jewish Reconstructionist Federation, 7804 Montgomery Ave., Elkins Park, PA 19027, (215) 782-8500.

Union of Orthodox Jewish Congregations of America, 45 West 36th Street, New York, NY 10018, (212) 563-4000.

There is one more branch asprouting with an appellation I feel is somewhat redundant because I believe all Jews are humanists. This is the **Society for Humanistic Judaism,** with thirty relatively new constituent congregations. On the other hand, although I hold a contrary opinion, there are those who define humanism as exclusive of prayer, making any notion of a "humanist" synagogue a self-contradiction. In any event, to see if there is such a congregation near you, call the Society at (248) 478-7600.

But perhaps even a "humanist" synagogue is too religious for you. If so, you still have other options that can offer many of the features synagogues provide (exclusive of prayer, of course), as well as characteristics uniquely their own.

Yes, I am pleased to report that the secular Jewish community is alive and well. Let's find out more about it.

CHAPTER
32

Jewish Secular Organizations

When I looked up the definition of "secular" in the dictionary, the first five meanings were expressed in the negative—secular is *not* religious, spiritual, or sacred; *not* belonging to religious orders; *non*-religious; and so on. Yet, it would be incorrect to think of secular Jews in terms of what they are not. And equally wrong to regard them as not caring about Jewish identity because there could be nothing further from the truth.

What does distinguish secular Jews from their religious counterparts is that for the most part, they do not believe in or have their doubts about God, prayer, and religious observances. But secular Jews do value Jewish history, our cultural heritage, the holidays, Jewish literature, and even the Bible. Moreover, secular Jewishness is something that has and continues to evolve.

A Jew who considered himself or herself secular a hundred years ago may have placed greater emphasis on Zionism or socialism as a means of expressing Jewishness than the secular Jew at the middle of the twentieth century who saw a mission in preserving the Yiddish language. Likewise, secular Jews today may be more concerned with providing an alternative Jewish education for their children in order to fortify Jewish identity against a tide of assimilation that did not exist two generations ago.

In the last twenty years, many secular Jews have found it appropriate to clarify how they are known with some preferring to add the word "humanist," thus calling themselves "secular humanistic Jews." After joining the Jewish Children's Folkshul in Philadelphia, I remember how I was part of the sometimes contentious debate about publicizing the school as offering a "secular and humanist" program in place of what had been described for four decades as "secular."

If you refer back to Part Three and glance at our Jewish values such as freedom, equality, iconoclasm, and the concept of "oneness," you'll readily see that you can fill your life with each and every one of these principles in a purely secular way. While you can do this on your own, there are also a number of Jewish secular/humanist organizations with which you may align yourself in strengthening your Jewish identity.

These groups offer a variety of opportunities. For one, with the growing concern about the loss of our Jewish identity and the need to furnish the next generation with meaningful and relevant reasons to remain Jewish, the primary purpose of many of these groups is to provide a Jewish secular education for children such as the Jewish Children's Folkshul in Philadelphia that my sons attended. We shall explore these opportunities in greater detail in Chapter 42.

But there are activities other than education for our children. For instance, some secular organizations remain concerned with the preservation of Yiddish and conduct programs dealing with Yiddishkeit and the Yiddish language.

Since historically, secular Jews rallied around the labor movement, civil rights, and other social issues, many of these groups still emphasize these concerns by providing social services or being politically active (see Chapters 33 and 34). It is not unusual to find teenagers from a Jewish secular school or spunky senior citizens belonging to a Jewish secular group boarding a bus taking them to the nation's capital to protest a war or atomic energy, or to march in support of civil liberties or a woman's right to choose.

Many of these organizations provide a forum for speakers and discussions on a wide range of subject-matter. A number have their own publications, several of which will appear in Chapter 37. There may be consideration given to issues involving Israel and topics confronting the Jewish community both local and worldwide. Speakers may lecture on Jewish history and culture as well as contemporary themes.

Though there are more Jewish secular/humanist groups offering a greater diversity of programs than a hundred years ago, it is not a large movement. An exception is **The Workmen's Circle/Arbeiter Ring** that boasts 24,000 members. Though The Workmen's Circle was founded to support the fledgling labor movement and still remains active with labor causes, it provides a variety of services to its members and conducts an assortment of activities including the promotion of Yiddish, Jewish cultural programs, schools for children, and housing for the elderly. Chapters are located in New York, Philadelphia, Boston, Michigan, Ohio, Toronto, and California. Information may be obtained from the national office: 45 Sholom Aleichem Pl. (E. 33rd Street), New York, NY 10016, (800) 922-2558.

Not long ago, a number of secular Jewish groups formed an umbrella association called the **Congress for Secular Jewish Organizations** (CSJO), whose member groups represent 900 families. To find out if there is one that interests you and is geographically convenient, contact the CSJO in care of its executive director, Roberta Feinstein, 19657 Villa Drive North, Southfield, MI 48067, (248) 569-8127.

Twenty secular Jewish organizations comprise the **North American Federation of Secular Humanistic Jews** which in turn is associated with the **International Federation of Secular Humanistic Jews** (888-252-4246). This confederation consists of member organizations in a number of countries including Israel, Russia, Canada, and the United States.

The best way to reach groups in the Federation is through the **North American Institute for Secular Humanistic Judaism,** 28611 West Twelve Mile Rd., Farmington Hills, MI 48334, (248) 476-9532.

Many secular Jewish organizations have specific agendas and therefore will be included in the chapters to follow. So, with that in mind, let's move on to what I like to call Jewish social service groups or "Jews helping others."

CHAPTER
33

Jews Helping Others—
Jewish Service Organizations

Hear the one about the comely young man who was stood up under the chuppah by his bride-to-be and now gazed with woeful eyes into the bleak waters by the docks in Haifa? As he was about to leap from the pier, a policeman happened by and, upon taking notice of the forlorn lad, he asked, "Why would someone in the prime of life as yourself want to end it all?"

"Because I don't want to live without my Deborah!"

"Well, that may be, mister," said the nervous officer, "but please don't jump in the water. You see, if you do, I must dive in after you to save you and I can't swim. And that means both of us will drown and I have a wife and three small children who depend upon me. Now, would you want that on your conscience? Of course not. So, be a good Jew and do a mitzvah and go home and hang yourself."

While Jews are sometimes referred to as the "People of the Book" (Chapter 35), it would be even more accurate to say we are the "People of the Mitzvah." One definition for the word mitzvah is "commandment" and *halakhah* is filled with 613 of them. These 613 commandments govern the lives of the most pious and observant Jews.

There is another definition for mitzvah that you may want to embrace. Mitzvah also means a meritorious act and, as a Jew, it is incumbent upon you to perform as many as you can.

Exactly what constitutes these meritorious acts? While the rabbis are fairly certain of the answer and over the centuries a body of rabbinical law has been compiled explaining this, I am not one to say with any degree of certainty. I leave it to you and your conscience.

Because the performing of mitzvoth is so deeply embedded into our Jewish value system, there are many Jewish organizations you can join to advance this objective. Now, you may ask, why need it be a Jewish organization? Why not nondenominational groups? Don't they perform good deeds as well?

Of course they do and you should feel free to associate yourself with any worthy cause you wish. I know I have. But there are Jewish groups performing mitzvoth for Jews and non-Jews alike and by working with these groups, you may find you realize two goals at the same time—fulfilling the responsibility to carry out mitzvoth and fortifying your Jewish identity.

In the 1970s, a grassroots movement began with the aim of *tikkun olam*—the "healing and transformation" of the world. This has become known as the Jewish Renewal movement and provides a Jewish response to issues involving peace, equality, poverty, and the environment. The Jewish Renewal movement has also taken on a religious dimension as exemplified by two of its founders who are now rabbis (though of the unconventional sort)—Rabbi Arthur Waskow and Rabbi Zalman Schacter-Shalomi.

If you wish to explore this fascinating approach to healing the world, contact **ALEPH: Alliance for Jewish Renewal,** 7318 Germantown Ave., Philadelphia, PA 19119, (215) 247-9700.

There are many other groups and organizations committed to acts of mitzvoth. Some of these are very well-established and will sound familiar like B'nai B'rith, with a quarter million members across the globe. Others may have a specific purpose such as providing comfort and care to the terminally ill and are staffed with a handful of volunteers.

Listed below is a sample of what you might discover should you wish to associate yourself with like-minded Jews and carry out the commandment to perform good deeds:

Association of Jewish Children's and Family Agencies. 3086 State Highway 27, Suite 11, P.O. Box 248, Kendall Park, NJ 08824, (800) 634-7346. The national association for local groups that provide services for the elderly, children, and those in need.

B'nai B'rith. 1640 Rhode Island Ave., N.W., Washington, DC 20036, (888) 388-4224. Promotes social justice, education, and service to the community.

Committee for Judaism and Social Justice. c/o *Tikkun*, 251 W. 100 Street, New York, NY 10025.

Jewish Fund for Justice. 1334 G Street, N.W., 3rd Floor, Washington, DC 20005. Supports economically and socially-culturally disadvantaged persons.

Jewish Healing Center. 1512 Granger Way Line, Redwood City, CA 94061. A Jewish hospice. [There are numerous Jewish hospices throughout the country.]

Jewish Women International. www.jewwomen.org. Jewish women committed to *tikkun olam*.

Mazon. A Jewish Response to Hunger. 2940 Westwood Blvd., Suite 7, Los Angeles, CA 90064.

National Jewish Coalition for Literacy. (212) 545-9215.

Shomrei Adamah. (215) 887-1988. Provides material on Judaism and the environment.

You may want to consider the **Jewish Federation** or **United Jewish Appeal** which finance many worthwhile social service agencies. They're not hard to find what with 184 Jewish federations across the country!

On the other hand, perhaps you have something less traditional and more political in mind. If this is the case, let's move on and see what we can do about it.

CHAPTER
34

Be Politically Active
Promoting Jewish Values

In 1892, two boys, both named David, were born to poor Jewish parents—one in Russian Poland, the other in Russia proper. Nineteen years later, they leave their shtetls in search of a better life and meet on the ship taking them to America.

Brimming with enthusiasm, the Davids become cloak cutters at a manufacturing company in Philadelphia. After years of toiling for subsistence wages in sweatshop conditions, their dreams turn into disillusionment. But instead of despairing, they determine to do something about it.

In 1922, the two Davids organize a strike. When they lose, they're blacklisted from working in the City of Brotherly Love. One David moves to New York. The other David finds work in Vineland, New Jersey, where he can support his wife and two sons. They bid each other well and go their separate ways.

When David Dubinsky arrived in New York, he joined the International Ladies Garment Workers Union (ILGWU). Ten years later, Dubinsky became president of the ILGWU, an office he held until 1966. The other David, my grandfather, died of tuberculosis in 1933.

The tale of the two Davids is the opening of a piece I wrote for the *Philadelphia Forum* entitled, "Calling All Real Liberals." The essay had to do with retrieving the "L" word (Liberalism), from the trash bin and restoring it as a badge to be worn with pride.

In this article, I refer to the following individuals as exemplars of liberalism, albeit in different decades and under different circumstances: Victor Rabinowitz, the indefatigable lawyer who, during a career spanning sixty years, defended strikers and trade union activists, people hauled before the House Un-American Activities Committee (HUAC), civil rights protesters, and Vietnam War draft resisters; Abbie Hoffman, the archetype of the 1960s "New Left" whose first foray into activism began with the Mississippi Freedom Summer Project in 1964; Paul Krassner and Jerry Rubin, who were at the forefront of the antiwar movement along with Hoffman and others.

Because the paper publishing my article had a general circulation, it was never my intention for all the individuals I cited to be Jewish. Nor would I ever imply Jews hold a monopoly on liberalism. But it's just that we have been disproportionately represented in causes attracting liberals which is probably due to our Jewish values (Chapters 13 and 14 in particular), and our activist tendencies (Chapter 18).

Further, I am in no way equating liberalism with being Jewish. I am only using this as an example of participating in the political arena. Many distinguished Jews, like Norman Podhoretz, are prominent in the neoconservative movement and in the Republican Party.

The point is that by taking a political stance in pursuit of your Jewish value system, you can bolster your Jewish identity and there are many Jewish organizations from which to choose. Some of these appeared in the previous pages, such as **The Workmen's Circle**, which seeks to establish a society "free from oppression, discrimination, and exploitation." In addition, there are other Jewish organizations I have not mentioned and two in particular may pique your interest.

The **American Jewish Congress** is dedicated to defending human rights and to assuring a humane and equitable future for all people. It also has acted as an advocate for Israel and Jews living in the former Soviet Union. Frequently, the American Jewish Congress aligns itself with similar groups in defending the Bill of Rights—the first ten amendments of our Constitution. To find out more about the American Jewish Congress, contact a regional office near you or the national office: 15 E. 84th Street, New York, NY 10028, (212) 879-4500.

The **Anti-Defamation League of B'nai B'rith** works to combat discrimination. Although the ADL is particularly concerned with anti-semitism, it takes stands against discrimination of all types and defends the civil, religious, educational, and economic rights of all citizens. For information, get in touch with a local office or the national office: 823 United Nations Plaza, New York, NY 10017, www.adl.org.

Of course, there are numerous nonsectarian organizations you may find appealing. And while they are not made up solely of Jews or promote specific Jewish causes as part of their agenda, it just may be that by becoming involved with one or more of these groups, you'll discover your Jewish identity being nurtured just the same.

How is this so? Simple. By providing an outlet in which you can actively pursue those Jewish values that are part of your natural inclination and in which you believe, you will feel yourself being more of a Jew.

But maybe organizations and groups are not for you. Or perhaps, you can take only so much at a time without becoming overwhelmed with committee meetings and board politics. Possibly, you're more cerebral and can think of nothing better than spending a few uninterrupted hours curled up with a good book or magazine that gives you pause to contemplate life and its myriad of mysteries.

Well then, guess what? This can be a great way to fortify your Jewish identity or discover it in the first place. With Jewish books and periodicals, it's like the tee shirt says—"So much to read and so little time."

So, let's move on to Part Eight.

Part VIII

Reading and Being Jewish Even on the Internet!

CHAPTER
35

After All,
We Are the "People of the Book"

One night in May 1933, the black canopy draped over Berlin was pierced by soaring flames. The bonfire below was fueled by a single source—Jewish books. Though written a century earlier, the words of Heinrich Heine, the great German poet of Jewish ancestry, proved prophetic: "Where they burn books they will also, in the end, burn human beings."

In the 1950s, Stalin's Soviet regime purged its Jewish poets and writers. Manuscripts were confiscated and Jewish men and women of letters were snatched away in the middle of the night and shot or imprisoned.

When I was assigned to write an article on Jewish Book Month and Jewish book festivals, I began with the preceding paragraphs. It was as if the two most evil men of the last century, and perhaps in recorded history, knew perfectly well that if one wanted to destroy the Jewish soul, one had to begin by burning the fodder that nourished and stoked it—Jewish books. For we are, after all, the "People of the Book."

Interestingly enough, while conducting interviews for the article, I learned how we came about this appellation, which was something I had always thought we Jews took upon ourselves. But not so. According to Arthur Kurzweil, president of Jewish Book News and Editor-in-Chief of Jason Aronson Inc., Publishers, it was the Muslims who dubbed the Hebrews the "People of the Book." This was the way, Kurzweil explained, the outside community viewed the Jews and has been ever since.

Why are we perceived in this fashion? Perhaps it goes back to the Five Books of Moses and the manner in which we have consistently venerated scholars who devote their lives to the study of Torah, Mishna, and Talmud. Not only are the books revered, but the words and Hebrew letters are considered sacred. Susan Gubar, author and professor of English, suggests that "a devotion to the book . . . may have been fostered by a religion based on reading, interpreting, blessing, kissing and parading classical Jewish texts. . . ."

Books have a special place in our history and this has cemented the bonds holding Jews together over the centuries—particularly in the Diaspora. But it also has helped to gather us when we returned to our homeland. Amos Oz is convinced that what brought Jews together from ninety-six different countries was a "common literary, liturgical and cultural tradition. Books are what brought them here [Israel]. The only unifying force [was] in their heads."

For some, like Cynthia Ozick, reading is the only expression of Jewishness:

> As a Jew I am an autodidact: the synagogue at present does not speak to me, and I have no divine shelter other than reading; at the moment print is all my Judaism. . . . My reading has become more and more urgent. . . . I read mainly to find out not what it is to be a Jew—my own life in its quotidian particulars tells me that—but what it is to think as a Jew.

Whether you take a position similar to Cynthia Ozick that "print is all my Judaism," or an approach that reading material of Jewish interest and content can be a part of your Jewishness, this is an excellent way to strengthen your identity as a Jew. While there are many ways to go about this, which we will discuss in the chapters to follow, we must first address a rather obvious question—what is it that makes a book or article or story "Jewish?"

The approach I take here is no different than the one I followed in Part Two when we grappled with the question—"Who is a Jew?" Admittedly, there are those who will say that anything other than Talmud and Mishna and the like are *trayf*. But those "authorities" more than likely consider me and this book *trayf*. So who cares? I prefer an all-inclusive notion of Jewish books and reading material. Whether the author is Jewish is only a minor factor. The more important consideration is the content.

To answer this, I draw a parallel to the way I discern good art—I know it when I see it. I think it's the same with Jewish reading material. It's really intuitive and as we proceed, I'd rather err on the side of inclusion than exclusion. So if at first glance, some material in these chapters or several of the books in the Appendix don't seem Jewish to you, maybe it wouldn't hurt to take another look.

Before moving on to Jewish books, however, I'd like to mention one organization you might find of interest. The **Jewish Book Council** conducts a number of programs and publishes *Jewish Book World*, a literary magazine, and the *Jewish Book Annual*. It also provides services to individuals and groups by offering assistance and information about the American Jewish literary scene. You may reach this organization at their national headquarters: 15 East 26 Street, New York, NY 10010, (212) 532-4949, ext. 297.

Now, on to Jewish books!

CHAPTER
36

Books of Jewish Interest—So Many!

Reading Jewish books is a wonderful way to strengthen your Jewish identity by learning the history of the Jewish people, what is occurring in the present, and what the future may hold as well as what we can do about it. It also provides a connection to the Jewish characters that populate the pages—real or imagined. As Henry Roth put it:

> Stories . . . told you how people felt, what they saw and heard, and how they lived. That was the important thing: They were part of a world, one that maybe didn't exist anymore, but that was the only way you could know it.

Because there isn't much difference between writers and readers, or as Saul Bellow suggests: "A writer is a reader moved to emulation." The mandate Elie Wiesel set for Jewish writers applies equally to Jewish readers: "It is incumbent upon the Jewish writer to be witness to all that has haunted the people of Israel from its beginnings."

Reading Jewish books provides innumerable opportunities to bear witness, learn about our People, and plan for the future. With hundreds of new books of Jewish interest published each year, there are many from which to choose. What is more, there are a variety of ways you can go about this.

If you remember, I began the previous chapter with the opening for an article I wrote about Jewish book festivals that occur during Jewish Book Month, the thirty-day period before Chanukah. For this event and the scores of Jewish book fairs held annually all over the country, we have Fanny Goldstein to thank. Fanny was a librarian in the Boston Public Library and in 1925, she displayed Jewish books during what she called Jewish book week.

While the Jewish Book Council, also mentioned in the preceding chapter, sponsors Jewish Book Month, most of the book fairs during that time are held under the auspices of Jewish community centers. These events vary but usually take place over a period of several days and include readings and signings by authors, exhibitions of Jewish books, and sometimes a banquet with distinguished speakers. To find out if there will be a Jewish book fair near you, watch for advertising, look for articles in the Jewish presses (next chapter), or contact your local Jewish community center or the **Jewish Community Centers Association,** 15 E. 26th Street, New York, NY, 10010, (212) 532-4949.

Now, if you are more sedentary and you'd rather browse in a comfortable armchair, you can consider a membership in the **Jewish Book Club.** By becoming a member, you will receive the *Jewish Book News,* a journal of essays and reviews with over 650 titles from more than 70 publishers. Like most book clubs, you can receive the main selection or choose from numerous alternate titles, many at discounts up to 90 percent. There are books on every conceivable topic of Jewish interest ranging from fiction to the Holocaust to holidays to women's studies and Jewish thought. For information, contact the Jewish Book Club at (610) 534-2884, fax (610) 532-9001 or email www.aronson.com.

On a global scale, **Vallentine Mitchell** is an international publisher of books of Jewish interest. For the current catalogue, contact the offices in the United Kingdom: phone: +44 (0) 181 599 8866; fax: +44 (0) 181 599 0984; email: jlegg@frankcass.com.

Perusing reviews of Jewish books is a great way to make a selection from the numerous titles. Another good reason to read reviews is that unless you are a voracious reader with unlimited time on your hands, it's not likely you'll get to read everything in which you have an interest. Book reviews provide a synopsis of the salient points you would otherwise miss.

It would take a book by itself to list all the American publishing houses of books with Jewish themes since almost every major publisher, and even many small ones, particularly university presses, publish both fiction and nonfiction of Jewish interest. However, there are a number of publishing houses that either exclusively publish Judaica or have a significant proportion of their books in this area. You may contact these publishers and request their current catalogue. In some cases, you can order directly from the publisher. Otherwise, it's to the book stores or the Internet. But remember, if you don't see what you are looking for, you can usually special-order the book.

At the end of this chapter, you will find most of these publishers of Judaica. An asterisk indicates a house which publishes Judaica exclusively or where it represents a major portion of its list.

But bear in mind there are many books of Jewish interest published by houses other than those listed below. Therefore, you should still keep your sights open for Jewish books in any of the ways I suggested above or by browsing through the section for Jewish books in book stores and libraries or surfing the internet.

* **Jason Aronson, Inc., Publishers.** 1-800-860-5122.
     www.aronson.com
Beacon Press. (617) 742-2110. www.beacon.org/Beacon.
Doubleday Religious Division. Fax # (212) 782-8911.
     www.bdd.com
* **Behrman House, Inc.** (201) 669-0447.
Harper San Francisco. (415) 477-4400. www.harpercollins.com
Harvard University Press. (617) 495-2600. www.hvp.harvard.edu.
Indiana University Press. (812) 855-4203.
* **Jewish Lights Publishing.** (802) 457-4000.
* **The Jewish Publication Society.** (215) 564-5925.
* **Kar-Ben Copies.** (301) 984-8733. www.karben.com.
* **Ktav Publishing.** (201) 963-9524.
* **Mesorah Publishing, Ltd.** (718) 921-9000.
Oxford University Press. (212) 726-6000.

Riverhead Books (imprint of Penguin Books). (212) 951-8400.
www.putnam.com

* **Schocken** (imprint of Knopf/Random House). (212) 751-2600.

Shambala Publications. (617) 424-0030.

* **Union of American Hebrew Congregations Press.**
(212) 249-0100.

CHAPTER
37

Jewish Periodicals and Tabloids

In the last chapter, I suggested how useful book reviews are not only as a resource to determine what you might want to add to your reading list but also to get the gist of those books you don't have time to read. The best place to find these reviews are in Jewish periodicals and tabloids where this is only one of the features these publications offer.

Jewish magazines fall into one of two categories. Many are published by an organization, like *Hadassah Magazine,* and therefore a significant portion of the content is dedicated to disseminate information or provide material of interest to their respective members. Some of these periodicals are inclined to exclude anything which would be inconsistent with their mission while others do not consider this to be a factor. Regardless, almost all these magazines contain material on a wide range of subject matter from travel to holidays to Jewish thought and book reviews. Consequently, you may find one or more of these publications to be of interest even if you do not belong to the parent organization.

Then we have periodicals such as *Moment,* that are independent of any specific Jewish group. Naturally, there is room for more editorial discretion and journalistic autonomy with these magazines. And yet sometimes, a specific ideology will prevail in the editorial board room so that *Commentary* might be more likely to reflect the neoconservatism of its editor, Norman Podhoretz, and *Tikkun*, that of its founder and leading proponent of Jewish Renewal, Michael Lerner.

None of which is to say that I am suggesting one type of magazine is superior to another. This is for you, the reader, to decide. But you should not be dissuaded from perusing the pages of a publication which may be sponsored by an organization in the fear it is nothing more than an official voice for that group.

A great way to find out what is going on in the Jewish community where you reside is to read the local Jewish newspaper, assuming there is one. Moreover, given our transient society, it is possible you have moved from your original home; subscribing to the Jewish newspaper where you once had lived will enable you to keep abreast of the life cycles and other goings-on regarding your former friends and acquaintances. In any event, reading Jewish newspapers is an easy and excellent method to strengthen your Jewish identity. If nothing else, it provides a sense of connection to the Jewish community.

Most Jewish tabloids appear weekly, while others less often. To my knowledge, the last daily Jewish newspaper was the Yiddish paper *Forverts* of decades ago, which is now the weekly *Forward*, published in English.

Like Jewish magazines, Jewish newspapers fall into two categories. Many are independent publications that generally cater to the local Jewish community. Although these independent papers have their share of announcements concerning regional events and milestones, they frequently include news articles from the wire services, opinion pieces and commentaries, literary sections, reviews of film and theater, and often general interest such as business, health, and travel.

The other category of Jewish newspapers consists of those published by the local Jewish federation. On the one hand, these tabloids resemble the independents but because they are frequently well-funded, they are sometimes more impressive, at least in number of pages. Thus, there is often more to read on both the national and international level and, of course, there will be everything you need to keep informed regarding what is going on in the local Jewish community—particularly federation functions.

There can be subtle distinctions between federation papers and the independents. For one, the former group is likely to provide more coverage pertaining to federation. Editorial integrity may also be compromised because federations are concerned with raising money and any federation sponsored publication is a valuable tool in this regard. Given the diversity of even the smallest Jewish community, these papers have to be careful not to antagonize contributors to the federation. Hence, something controversial might not see print in some of these papers. On the other hand, you may find the editorial pages contain lively debate as these papers want to maintain goodwill among all segments of the Jewish community and thus offer a forum to every side of a question.

Frankly, finding Jewish magazines isn't always easy. Some can be purchased at book stores or are available in libraries (especially university or Jewish libraries). Many Jewish publications have their own web site that you can visit on the internet. But remember, even if you don't want to belong to an organization, you can still call and see what it would cost to subscribe to its periodical or perhaps request a sample copy to examine. And while federations frequently make their papers available free to contributors, they can also be purchased with a subscription.

I wish to emphasize that the list below by no means contains *all* Jewish magazines and tabloids. If you have difficulty determining the Jewish newspaper serving your community, there are two helpful sources: **Jewish Media List** at www.libertynet.org indexes Jewish print publications devoted to reporting Jewish news; **Jewish Publications at Zipple,** at www.zipple.com, lists Jewish newspapers and periodicals.

MAGAZINES OF JEWISH INTEREST

Agada. (510) 848-0965. Jewish experience, values, fiction, poetry, essays.

Amit. (212) 477-4720. Articles of interest to Jewish women, Israel, holidays, travel.

The B'nai B'rith International Jewish Monthly. (202) 857-6645. Jewish affairs.

Commentary. (212) 751-4000. Culture, literary, Jewish affairs.

Congress Monthly. (212) 879-4500. Published by American Jewish Congress. Topics of concern to the American Jewish community.

Hadassah Magazine. (212) 333-5946. General interest, Jewish affairs, and literature.

Inside. (215) 893-5700. Contemporary quarterly magazine of Jewish interest and lifestyle.

Israel Horizons, Progressive Zionist Quarterly. (212) 868-0377. Israel and the American Jewish community.

Jewish Currents. (212) 924-5740. Jewish secularism, history, Israel, Yiddish culture.

Midstream. (212) 339-6040. Zionist, Jewish interest, literary, Jewish thought.

Moment, The Magazine of Jewish Culture & Opinion. (202) 364-3300. General Jewish interest, political, historical, religious, lifestyle.

Na'amat Woman of Na'amat USA. (212) 725-8010. Jewish and Israeli themes and issues.

Reconstructionist. (215) 887-1988. Jewish interest, public policy, religious studies.

Reform Judaism. (212) 650-4240. Reform Jewish issues.

The Reporter. (212) 505-7700. Published by Women's American ORT. Jewish topics, social issues, education, the Middle East, and women.

Sh'ma, A Publication of Jewish Family and Life. (781) 449-9894. A forum for dialogue on Jewish topics.

Tikkun. Literary, Jewish thought, Jewish renewal.

United Synagogue Review. Issues of concern to Conservative Jewish community.

JEWISH NEWSPAPERS

Akron Jewish News. (330) 869-2424.

American Jewish World. (612) 920-7000. (Minneapolis).

Connecticut Jewish Ledger. (203) 231-2424.

Detroit Jewish News. (248) 354-6060.

Forward. (800) 849-1825. General Jewish interest, literary, local (NY), but much national and international Jewish news.

Heritage Florida Jewish News. (407) 834-8787.

Heritage Southwest Jewish Press. (213) 737-2122 (Los Angeles).

The Jewish Advocate. www.neponsent.com. (Boston & parts of New England).

Jewish Bulletin in San Francisco. http://gort.used.edu

Jewish Exponent. (215) 893-5710. Published by Jewish Federation of Greater Philadelphia.

Jewish News. (216) 991-8300. (Cleveland).

Jewish News of Greater Phoenix. (602) 870-9470.

Jewish News of Western Massachusetts. (413) 582-9870.

The Jewish Post of New York. www.jewishpost.com

Jewish Press. (402) 334-6449. Published by Jewish Federation of Omaha.

Jewish Press. (800) 992-1600. (Brooklyn).

Jewish Times of the South Jersey Seashore. (609) 407-0909.

The Jewish Week. (212) 921-7822. (New York).

Jerusalem Post Newspaper. www.jpost.com. Israeli paper published in English.

St. Louis Jewish Light. (314) 432-3353.

San Diego Jewish Times. (619) 463-5575.

Savannah Jewish News. (912) 355-8111.

Washington Jewish Week. (301) 230-2222.

CHAPTER
38

Surf Jewish on the Internet—
Jewish Web Sites

When I first went online and surfed the Internet, which wasn't until the turn of the millennium, I was astonished to see there were 6,482 one hundred percent Jewish web sites! Even more astounding, there were a quarter million web sites containing some Jewish content! And of course, the number (web sites that is, unfortunately not Jews), is constantly growing.

It is not my purpose to promote the value of the Internet, but it seems to me it offers an easy and convenient opportunity for you to investigate whatever it is that may be of interest to you concerning your Jewishness. And if not for you, perhaps you may find it an excellent means for your children or grandchildren to utilize in exploring their Jewish identity especially since they constitute the generations where computers play such an integral part of their lives.

In fact, this is already happening. Consider the web site known as Jewishfamily.com. An estimated 70 percent of its 1,000 daily visitors are under 45 years old. Moreover, about a third of these are involved in interfaith relationships. It already appears the Internet is being used by young people who are looking for something to bolster their Jewish identity.

As I said, with so many thousands of Jewish web sites, I am not in a position to provide anything remotely resembling a listing of what is out there in cyberspace. However, the sites appearing below should give you a flavor of the diversity from which you can choose.

Quite literally, there is something for everyone, so the next time you're surfing on the net, why not stop and visit a Jewish web site or two that piques your interest. Just another way to maintain your Jewish identity.

FAMILY:

Jewish Family Life & Homepage. www.jewishfamily.com. 20 sites covering all aspects of Jewish life including food, health, parenting, books, and more.

Jewish Gen: The Official Home of Jewish Genealogy. www.jewish gen.org

Mishpacha. www.mishpacha.org. An introductory guide to Jewish life for parents wanting to build Jewish identity in their family.

FOOD:

Jewish Food Recipes Archives. www.jewishfood.org
Jewish Holiday Kitchen. www.epicurious.com
The Jewish Vegan Lifestyle. www.jewishvegan.com

JUDAICA:

Jewish Source. www.jewishsource.com. For things Jewish—books, jewelry, art, etc.

Judaism and Jewish Resources—Andrew Tannenbaum. http:// shamash.org. Popular and well organized index of things Jewish.

www.jewish.com/store Jewish gift shop.

HOLIDAYS:

B'nai B'rith Calendar of Jewish Holidays. http://bnaibrith.org
CyberSeder. www.emanuelnyc.org. Temple Emmanuel's (New York) web site broadcasting Passover rituals.

LITERARY/NEWS:

Jason Aronson Publishers, Inc. www.aronson.com. More than 650 Jewish titles available to be purchased on line.
Jewishfamily.com. www.jewishfamily.com. Jewish magazine.
Jewish World Review. www.jewishworldreview.com. Magazine.
Muskeljuden. www.westegg.co./muskeljuden. Semisatirical cyber space magazine devoted to rethinking the Jewish past, present, and future.

ORGANIZATIONS:

Jewish Feminist Resources. http://world.std.com
Jewish Women International. www.jewishwomen.org. Jewish women committed to *tikkun olam* (repairing the world).
World Congress of Gay & Lesbian Jewish Organizations. www.vwc.edu. Information on its sixty-five member groups.
The American Israel Public Affairs Committee. www.aipac.org

MISCELLANEOUS:

Jewish Celebrations—the Jewish Wedding Resources & Planning. www.mazomet.com
Jewish Funerals, Burials, and Mourning. http://users.erols.com/zinner
Jewish Music Home Page. www.jewishmusic.com. Lists artists, articles, and links to other Jewish music web sites.
Jewish Travel. www.jewishtravel.com. How to find synagogues, kosher restaurants, and so forth when you are traveling.
Jewish Women's Archive. www.jwa.org. Historical record of Jewish women.

JStudies.Org—Our Jewish Studies Site. www.JStudies.org. Site for Jewish studies including institutions, bibliographies, scholars, and links.

Single Jew Jewish Singles Dating Site With Photos. www.singlejew. com

The National Yiddish Book Center. www.yiddishbooks.com

Yihud: The Jewish Meditation web site. http://rashi.tiac.net/yihud/ index.html

PART IX

Adult Education

CHAPTER
39

Learn About Being Jewish
with the Mind of an Adult

Imagine if you had stopped your education before entering high school. What sort of comprehension and appreciation would you have for your country's history, government, and values? You'd find yourself with the mind of a twelve-year-old forced to think in terms of "either–or," unable to grasp the subtleties and intricacies of this world of ours. You would have to believe in the tale of young George Washington and the cherry tree or else reject it outright and conclude all presidents are liars. Either Indians would have deserved to be slaughtered in the name of "manifest destiny" or they were always innocent victims who never raised a fist in anger. If the Civil War was not all about freeing the slaves, then doesn't that make Abraham Lincoln just one more deceptive politician plucking the heart strings of the abolitionists for votes?

With Jewish thought, history, culture, and religion, it is no different. Things are not always in black and white nor so simple, and for Jewish education to cease after a bar/bat mitzvah when a child turns thirteen means we will have a Jewish population basically ignorant concerning our Jewishness. And to a large extent, I regretfully submit, this is precisely the case today and one of the main causes for our diminishing numbers.

Faced with this "either–or" scenario concomitant with a juvenile education, many Jewish adults forego their Jewishness. If they can no longer give credence to the Hebrew tales and biblical miracles, then the Hebrew Bible must be worthless. If they can no longer believe in a deity to whom prayers can be addressed and from whom answers are forthcoming, then God must be rejected. If they can no longer accept the 613 oral directives issued by God to Moses, then all Jewish traditions and customs must be abandoned.

Obviously, the answer to correct this situation is for Jewish education to be continued past the bar/bat mitzvah age and even beyond confirmation. A meaningful Jewish education for our children is invaluable to help ensure they maintain their Jewish identity and we will explore this in Chapter 42. But equally vital, and particularly for those of us whose Jewish schooling was terminated at an early age or the quality left something to be desired, there is a pressing need to learn about Jewishness with the mature mind.

If we travel just a bit back in our past to pre-Nazi Germany, we will see circumstances not dissimilar from what we have in the United States today. Assimilation was threatening to destroy Jewish identity. Ironically, had it not been for Hitler and Nazism foisting Jewishness upon Jews who were otherwise disposed to discard it, Jewish identity might have succumbed entirely to the onslaught of assimilation in the open society Germany had briefly become.

To combat this threat of the "vanishing German Jew," two Jewish scholars and philosophers, Martin Buber and Franz Rosenzweig, established the "Judische Lehrhaus" in 1920, which was designed to be a dynamic pedagogy introducing assimilated Jews to classic Hebrew texts, Jewish literature, and philosophy. After Rosenzweig's premature death in 1929, the Lehrhause closed but was reopened by Buber in 1933 as the Frankfurt Lehrhaus under the auspices of the Center for Jewish Adult Education in an effort to support the beleaguered Jewish community. This school attracted many great scholars as teachers including Abraham Joshua Heschel.

Men like Buber, Rosenzweig, and Heschel knew that the survival of the Jewish people depended upon an adult Jewish populace that was well-informed in the ways of its heritage. But to fully appreciate why this is so, one must understand that a "Jewish" education means more than learning about Jewishness. It encompasses the manner in which the material is conveyed and the critical thinking required of the student. The ability to think independently is essential in order for one to appreciate and further our Jewish values. This is why education has always been highly regarded by us Jews.

For instance, consider what some Jews have observed about this topic.

The advancement of learning is the highest commandment.
—Maimonides

Whoever teaches his son teaches not alone his son but also his son's son, and so on to the end of generations.
—The Talmud

The true educator is not one who simply teaches, but one who teaches a child to think for himself.
—Rabbi Menachem Mendel Schneerson

All true education is help toward self-discovery and toward self-unfolding.
—Martin Buber

Learning-learning-learning: that is the secret of Jewish survival.
—Ahad Haam.

Ahad Ha'am had it right. Becoming learned in things Jewish will not only fortify your own Jewish identity but enable you to convey its value in an intelligent manner to others—particularly your children and grandchildren (Chapter 41). In this fashion, we can help assure a continuation of our Jewish values for future generations.

Now, how to go about this? Fortunately, there is a myriad of Jewish subjects from which you can choose and many forums in which to learn about them, as the next chapter will demonstrate.

CHAPTER
40

Where to Go to Learn

Remember in Chapter 30, I began with the piece I wrote for *Midstream*, titled *Train to Nowhere*, and near the end I repeated the Yiddish song my bubbe used to sing to me, *"Wie ahin zul ich gayn?,"* "Where shall I go?" Well, for us Jews, that has often been a life and death dilemma for the better part of the last two millennia and no more so than the middle of the twentieth century in Nazi dominated Europe. Fortunately, when it comes to learning about things Jewish, there is a plethora of answers to the question, "Where shall I go?"

But first, a word about the subject matter. If you think you are limited to learning the same things you were taught in Hebrew school where you may have paid scant attention, think again. Sure, there is the Bible and Jewish history; however, as the previous chapter stressed, now you will be instructed as an adult. Of course, there is also the Hebrew language but in addition to studying it as the vernacular for prayer, it is taught as conversational Hebrew spoken by our fellow Jews living in Israel.

Then there is the myriad of subjects which was likely unavailable to you as a youngster attending Hebrew school. You can receive instruction in Talmud and Jewish philosophy. You can learn about Jewish recipes and cooking for the holidays as well as other traditions and ways to celebrate special occasions. In addition to Hebrew, you can become fluent in Yiddish at Yiddish centers and other institutions offering an opportunity to participate in the rebirth of this previously "dying" tongue. You can learn about Jewish mysticism and Kabbalah, Jewish spirituality and meditation, and the Jewish attitude toward death, dying, and an afterlife. Many courses or evenings are focused on books facilitated by the author, a book reviewer, or other leader. And all this is only a smidgen of what is accessible to you.

Now, as for where to go, here you also have numerous choices. Naturally, as you would expect, synagogues are a logical option even if you have no intention of attending prayer services. The same procedure applies here as indicated in Chapter 31 regarding selecting a synagogue. You can either contact individual congregations or their respective umbrella organizations.

You will find synagogues have a variety of offerings ranging from weekly Torah study with the rabbi to discussion groups to speakers. Just about every synagogue will be happy to provide the required education to enable you to become a bar or bat mitzvah if you missed out on this in your youth. You are never too old for this milestone. Recently, a cousin of mine had her bat mitzvah after turning eighty!

Some secular Jewish organizations (see Chapter 32) focus almost exclusively on education but almost all provide instruction in selected subjects. And while, as you might expect, much will be taught in the way of Jewish history, culture, and Yiddish, there are opportunities to study the Bible and other traditional Jewish tomes from a secular and modern perspective.

In Chapter 36, we learned Jewish book fairs are usually sponsored by local Jewish community centers. In addition to social activities, Jewish community centers frequently offer adult continuing education and enrichment programs, educational trips, and lectures. Feel free to contact your local Jewish community center in this regard or the Jewish Community Centers Association, the national umbrella organization in New York (see Chapter 36).

Now if it is small and intimate you prefer, I recommend looking into the Havurah movement. As indicated in Chapter 31, these groups sometimes conduct prayer services and may have a social component. But the thrust of the Havurah movement is education and many havurot do not even have religious rituals. Often, the group meets periodically in a member's home, a guest lecturer makes a presentation, and discussion follows. Informality is generally the rule but you can almost always be assured an enlightening time. If you do not know of a havurah near you, contact the **National Havurah Committee,** 7318 Germantown Avenue, Phila., PA 19119, (215) 248-9760.

When I was an undergraduate at Temple University in the second half of the sixties, my minor was religion and I took all the courses the department offered having to do with Jewishness—all two of them! Now, this was not because Temple had an inferior religion department—quite the contrary, it was well-respected. It simply reflected the sentiment that Jewish studies meant Judaism—the religion—and this was essentially the province of rabbis.

Today, this is not the case at all. In the Philadelphia area, for example, in addition to Temple, the University of Pennsylvania, Bryn Mawr College, and Haverford College offer undergraduate degrees with a concentration in Jewish studies. Nor do you have to matriculate. Many colleges and universities will allow you to audit a course or attend noncredit and personal enrichment courses, some of which will be in the area of Jewish studies, Judaica, the Middle East, and so on. There also are nondenominational or Jewish colleges specifically for Jewish studies that offer bachelor's and master's degrees as well as teaching certificates.

With so many options, you have no excuse to remain ignorant of your Jewish heritage. And if you truly care about your Jewish identity and the continuity of the Jewish people, you should avail yourself of at least some of the opportunities open to you.

So now that you're all set regarding how you can maintain your Jewish identity, one critical question remains—perhaps the most crucial of all the issues we have confronted thus far. Let's take a hard and honest look at the next generation—our kids and our grandchildren. For if we fail here, there is no future for us Jews or our Jewish values.

Part X

The Next Generation—
Your Children

CHAPTER
41

Be an Example!

Would you think of admonishing someone on the health hazard of smoking with a cigarette dangling from your lips? How about telling your kids they shouldn't drink and drive as you slide behind the wheel of your car after a dinner where you imbibed three martinis? Or lauding equality and tolerance as indispensable to a free society yet you pound a "for sale" sign into the front lawn of your home when a house on the block is sold to an African American? Would you really expect anyone to take you seriously in any of these situations?

Of course you wouldn't. And the same holds true regarding your Jewishness. If you gripe about the annual dues for a synagogue membership or the cost of tickets to gain admission on the high holidays and use this as an excuse never to attend a service, don't expect your children to pay you any attention when you question them regarding their absence from synagogue. If you can't read or understand a word of Hebrew, why should they be forced to set aside one or two afternoons a week and part of the weekend from their busy schedules to learn an "archaic" language? If you never visited Israel or supported even one of the many worthy projects undertaken there, why would you expect your kids to feel any affinity toward the Jewish homeland?

If being Jewish to you is no more than a convenient mantle of identity you assume whenever it happens to suit you, don't count on your children attaching any significance to their Jewish heritage. It just won't do to say to the next generation, "Do as I say, not as I do," in terms of being a Jew. And what is more, it would be a sad state of affairs if our kids did, in fact, meekly follow such a mandate.

Remember in Part Three when we talked about Jewish values and more particularly, Chapter 10 that explained how we Jews are independent thinkers? That's how our kids should be and to tell them they must go to synagogue or fast on Yom Kippur or not marry out of the faith without giving them a good reason, simply won't and shouldn't carry any weight with them. You have to furnish explanations and the best way to do this—better than any books or schooling or lecturing—is by your example.

Now, how do you go about being a model for your children to emulate? Well, for starters, in a sense, you don't.

Sounds like I've just contradicted myself, doesn't it? After saying you must provide an example for a Jewish life, it seems I've done a one hundred and eighty degree about-turn. Allow me to explain.

This may be a strong idiosyncrasy of mine but I firmly believe it to be in the Jewish tradition that every Jew must think independently. Suppose Abraham had followed the example of his father? Then we'd still be idolaters today and for all intents and purposes, there would be no Jews at all. But Abraham thought for himself and struck out on his own. So it should be with our children.

What you can and ought to do—and this is what I mean by serving as a role model—is to take your Jewishness to heart. Whatever you accept, or even reject, from Jewish tradition should be done without hypocrisy and with a deep sense of commitment.

Exactly how do you go about being a role model? Well, I would hope that if you've come along with me this far in the book, you realize there are many ways to accomplish this. Just pick and choose and feel free to change course whenever it seems appropriate and the right thing for you. Being Jewish can mean so many different things but whatever you embrace should be carried out with *Kavvanah*— fully focused and with your whole being.

One last caveat. Do not be troubled if your children or grandchildren reject your idea of what it is to be Jewish. What is important is that they emulate you in terms of your sincerity and caring for your

Jewish identity. Once they perceive this, they will chart their own course as a Jew.

What you can do to aid them in this regard is to offer opportunities to accomplish this. Thankfully, there are many diverse resources and venues for them as we shall see in Chapter 42.

CHAPTER
42

Resources:
Schools, Organizations, Activities

For whatever reason, when my younger son, Ari, approached the teen years, he had practically no Jewish friends despite living in a neighborhood and attending a school with significant Jewish populations. But later, this would change and he began having Jewish friends, some of whom, along with non-Jewish friends, form his closest circle of friends today. How did this come about?

It began when Ari was fourteen. His older brother, Cory, conscripted him to join the AZA chapter (Aleph Zadek Aleph of B'nai B'rith Youth Organization), that Cory had founded and of which he served as president. Ari joined and ultimately became president of Philadelphia Region AZA, twenty-seven years after I had held the same position.

None of which is to say that as a result of his four years in AZA, Ari has become anything even remotely resembling "super Jew," but it did provide him with a positive image of his Jewish identity and, as I said, bonded him to contemporaries with the same heritage. Thus, in addition to furnishing a formal education for your children, whether a full time Jewish day school or a few hours a week at a

Jewish secular school, you should realize there are many other opportunities to reinforce the Jewish identity of future generations.

Before I list some of these options, allow me to repeat the old adage, "You can lead a horse to water but you can't make him drink." With kids, and especially teenage kids, this goes double—no, make that triple! Despite my own personal enrichment from having been in AZA, I had only mentioned in passing to my sons that it was something that might interest them. Cory joined AZA on his own and, as I said, he's the one who drafted Ari.

While this is not a "parenting" book, nonetheless I respectfully suggest you refrain from barking commands ordering your children, especially the teenagers, to engage in this or that Jewish activity. Make them aware of the options and at the very least, even concerning their formative education, allow them to be part of the decision-making process.

With this in mind, below is a sample menu of the choices in the area of Jewish education, camps, and organizations. Although you can usually find local offices or affiliates in the customary manner, I will generally provide the national office you may contact. And remember, by no means is this an exhaustive compilation nor am I suggesting the superiority of one group or school over another.

EDUCATION:

Synagogues: Select as you would a synagogue. See Chapter 31.

Jewish Secular Schools: Most of the Jewish secular organizations, such as the Workmen's Circle, sponsor schools or have educational programs. See Chapter 32.

Jewish Day Schools: These are full-time private alternatives to public schools, combining a Jewish and secular education. Such schools are becoming increasingly popular and in 1999 185,000 students attended these schools located in 38 states and the District of Columbia. While most are Orthodox, many have been recently opened which are affiliated with the Conservative and Reform movements.

Jewish Community Centers: National umbrella group—Jewish

Community Centers' Association, (212) 532–4949. These centers frequently provide after-school enrichment programs.

Independent Hebrew Schools: Varies from locale to locale. Look for advertisements in your local Jewish publication, especially early in September.

Independent Jewish high schools and colleges: Unique to each community. Again, check out the advertisements.

YOUTH AND YOUNG ADULT ORGANIZATIONS:

B'nai B'rith Youth Organization: Contact the regional BBYO office or B'nai B'rith, (888) 388–4224. AZA for boys and BBG for girls, 9th through 12th grade. Provides leadership training, cultural, community service, Jewish identity, religion, social, and athletic activities.

Habonim/Dror North America: National Office—(212) 255–1796. Labor Zionist youth movement for ages 9–16, emphasizes social responsibility and offers programs in Israel.

Hillel, The Foundation for Jewish Campus Life: 1640 Rhode Island Ave., N.W., Washington, DC. Hillel has a presence on many college campuses providing a panoply of programs and holiday observances. (Although I promised no endorsements, this is a "no brainer" for you to suggest to your college-aged son or daughter.)

North American Federation of Temple Youth: Sponsored by Union of American Hebrew Congregations (Reform), (212) 650–4000. For high school teens promoting social action, culture and history of Judaism, social events.

United Synagogue Youth (USY): Sponsored by United Synagogue of Conservative Judaism, (215) 635–9701, but feel free to contact your local conservative synagogue. For high school teens offering programs in Jewish observances, volunteer work, and education.

Young Judaea: (215) 545–6270. Zionist youth organization for grades 4–12 and college age. Promotes Jewish heritage and Israel culture including trips to Israel.

CAMPS AND SUMMER PROGRAMS:

Day Camps: Jewish Community Centers often sponsor summer day camp programs with Jewish content. In addition, there are a number of independently owned Jewish day camps.

B'nai B'rith Perlman Camp: Located in Starlight, Pennsylvania. Call 800–270–7375 or www.bnaibrith.org/bbyo/perlman. BBYO also sponsors summer programs including trips to Israel.

Brandeis University: Four-week program for high school students integrating the humanities, arts, Jewish studies, and community service.

Camp Ramah in the Poconos: Located in the Pocono Mountains of Pennsylvania, this is a Conservative sponsored camp. (215) 885–8556.

Camp Shomira: Located in Liberty, NY, and operated under the auspices of Hashomer Hatzair, (215) 561–2446.

Camp Young Judaea: Located in Verbank, NY, and affiliated with Hadassah.

Summer Trips and Programs in Israel: Almost all Jewish youth organizations have such programs. In addition, synagogues, Zionist organizations, and Jewish federations conduct trips to Israel.

The choices are numerous. Never before in the history of Jews in the United States have there been so many opportunities for our young people to discover or reinforce their Jewishness. From traditional and observant Jewish programs to secular and cultural offerings, there is something for everyone. And while I did say you can lead a horse to water but can't compel him to drink, someone still has to lead the horse to the water! This is where you come in. Make certain your children are aware of these options.

Of course, there is no guarantee to what extent Jewish identity will be instilled or to what degree reinforced. And since love is blind, even a young adult with a very strong Jewish identity may fall in love with someone who is not Jewish. In fact, if current statistics hold, unless you are Orthodox, if you have four children, three of them will marry someone non-Jewish.

And if this should happen, what do you do? Let's take a look at Chapter 43.

CHAPTER
43

The Question of Intermarriage

Remember in *Fiddler on the Roof*, every time Tevye faced a dilemma, he'd lumber off and weigh the pros and cons, pondering, "On the one hand . . . but on the other hand . . ."? Generally, he was confronting challenges to tradition. First, one of his daughters wanted to marry someone other than the man he had selected. Later, another daughter didn't even bother to secure his permission to marry. Yet somehow, Tevye always came down on the side of his daughters and rationalized tradition away.

But when one daughter wanted to marry a Gentile, that was too much for poor Tevye and the love for his daughter could not outweigh tradition when balanced on the moral scales of a simple Jewish dairyman. Here Tevye drew the line. For Tevye, there was no "other hand" to consider when it came to intermarriage.

If Tevye were confronted with this dilemma today and still reached the same decision, he might find himself declaring almost all his daughters "dead to him." This is because studies have found that American Jews have intermarried at a rate of 50 percent and if you remove the Orthodox from the equation, the number of intermarriages in some surveys approaches 80 percent! Even more disturbing is what was disclosed by the National Jewish Population Survey, sponsored by the Council of Jewish Federations, which discovered that in addition to a 52 percent incidence of intermarriage, only one-quarter of the children of mixed marriages were raised as Jews.

Thus, it is more likely than not, your daughter-in-law or son-in-law will not be Jewish and almost a certainty, unless a dramatic shift in the trends occurs, most of your grandchildren will not be Jewish. Where Tevye agonized over repudiating one daughter who chose a non-Jewish spouse, you will be faced with disavowing practically your entire *mishpocheh*!

There is another reason to adopt a more receptive stance when it comes to this issue. Instead of viewing each marriage between Jew and Gentile as a loss for the Jewish people, it can be taken as a challenge to increase our numbers. Unfortunately, this is a contest we are abysmally losing.

In part, this is because the parents of the Jewish partner in an intermarriage are not doing nearly as good a job in conveying their Jewish values and identity to the grandchildren as the gentile grandparents are in transmitting their religions. Hebrew Union College researcher Bruce Phillips concluded in his study, "Children of Intermarriage: How Jewish?" that the efforts by the Jewish grandparents had no influence on the religion of the children while the efforts of grandparents to have the children raised as Christians reduced the proportion raised as Jews by nearly half.

Rather than losing the children of these unions, we should be seeking to absorb them into the Jewish community. Clearly, one way to accomplish this is to make both spouses welcome. Why, just consider, if we can change the 25 percent of the children currently brought up Jewish to 51 percent or more, the net effect would be an increase, rather than a decrease, of our Jewish population! This conclusion is supported by research conducted by a demographer at the University of Miami, Ira Sheskin, indicating that in some communities with ambitious outreach programs to interfaith couples, as many as two-thirds of the children of such marriages are raised Jewish while in those communities where little or no similar effort is made, as few as one in five of these children are raised as Jews.

Fortunately, it is easier to welcome a non-Jewish spouse into the Jewish community than ever before. The Reform and Reconstructionist movements have come to recognize patrilineal descent: the children of a Jewish father and non-Jewish mother (as has been with a Jewish mother and gentile father), are considered Jews and thereby entitled to a Jewish education, bar/bat mitzvah, and so on. These denominations of the Jewish community, while certainly not encouraging intermarriage, have become more tolerant of these relationships, and in many cases they have outreach programs in place.

Unfortunately, the Conservative branch is somewhat schizophrenic when it comes to this issue. On the one hand, cognizant of the statistics, it tries to be more amenable to interfaith unions and yet, at other times, presents a condescending, if not hostile, posture. For example, consider a recent decision of the Rabbinical Assembly's Committee on Law and Standards which declared Jews with a non-Jewish spouse should be barred from positions in synagogues where they may be perceived as role models.

So, exactly what do you do when faced with an impending marriage between your son or daughter and a Gentile intended-to-be? Or, for that matter, if you decide to marry someone who is not Jewish? One possibility, though occurring sporadically, is for the non-Jewish party to convert.

There is a distinct advantage to this. First, it is held by nearly all experts on child rearing that it is best and less confusing to raise a child in one religion. Moreover, studies have shown children raised in conversionary households are more likely to be brought up Jewish. One reason is that it is not unusual for the party converting to Judaism to become involved in the Jewish community and even more observant than the Jewish spouse.

If conversion is elected, you will have to do this in accordance with the requirements of the branch of Judaism you select. As you might expect, this is a more exacting process with the Orthodox and Conservative movements than the Reform and Reconstructionist. Contact the local board of rabbis, any synagogue, or national umbrella organization (see Chapter 31). As a resource book, you may wish to look at *Questions and Answers on Conversion to Judaism*, by Lawrence J. Epstein (Jason Aronson Publishers).

But even if conversion is only a possibility, a good start would be to approach one of the many programs that provide Jewish education to adults so the non-Jewish spouse can learn something about Jewishness. There may be outreach programs and interfaith networks in your community that offer educational seminars and courses. While not specifically designed for the conversion process, as the Greater Miami Jewish Federation's outreach program has shown, what begins as a mere interest in learning about things Jewish can culminate in a full-fledged conversion. On the secular side, you might consider the Intermarriage Department of the International Institute for Secular Humanistic Judaism with a toll free phone number, (888) 252–4246.

All this said, more likely than not, a conversion or even a fairly rigorous Jewish education is not likely to take place before the marriage. This then brings you to the matter of the wedding ceremony with one party who is not Jewish having little or no desire to become so, and the Jewish partner not inclined to be very observant. What kind of ceremony do you conduct under these circumstances? That's up to you, but allow me to share my thoughts on the type of ceremony *not* to hold.

Not long ago, my wife and I attended a spate of interfaith weddings. One in particular struck me where the bride was Jewish and a judge presided. I wrote a piece about it which was published as *Shelby's Wedding—An Interfaith Maze*, appearing in the *Heritage Florida Jewish News*. Here's how I described the ceremony:

> *His Honor blared the introductory remarks through beefy lips set in a beet red Irish face with all the emotions he probably possessed when arraigning a horde of hookers corralled after a midnight sweep of the streets. But then he settled in and when he recited by heart a lengthy poem of love and commitment, I was touched.*
>
> *Throughout the brief ceremony, he made veiled references to "traditions" but he never identified whose traditions we were witnessing or for what reason they were performed in the first place. I didn't have a clue why candles were lit (it wasn't Friday night), until my wife informed me it had to do with the Catholic service. Of course, I knew where the breaking of the glass came from as it shattered under the Italian groom's heel, but I did miss the customary explanations generally offered as to why Jews kept on doing this.*

I certainly don't mean to be critical of the cornucopia of customs but why the need to sanitize them? What's wrong in saying the "J" word (Jewish), or the "C" word (Catholic), with their respective rites? Of course, if the intention is to completely obliterate any reference to religion or heritage, it makes sense. But then why bother throwing in these rituals in the first place? It only leads to confusion. Which is exactly what happened at Shelby's wedding. Let me explain.

Well after the main meal, when everyone was about as imbibed as they were going to be, a group of women formed a chorus line and kicked their heels in the air. One shoe accidentally slipped off its high-flying foot and when it flew across the dance floor, almost hitting the band leader in the head, a hearty laughter welled from the assembly. Not about to be outdone, each woman in the chorus removed one shoe, setting it sailing helter-skelter.

Now, observing this with a studied expression was the fiancé of Shelby's brother. Knitting her eyebrows, she knew, also being Italian Catholic, this was not a custom of her people and therefore, not likely coming from the groom's contingent of the wedding. The fact that most of the women prancing with only one shoe were from Shelby's side of the room, led her to presume this was one more esoteric Jewish tradition. So the young lady took off her shoe and to the surprise of those around her, she flung it into the center of the dance floor shrieking "Matzal tough!" After all, she must have concluded, soon she would be the bride in one more interfaith wedding so why not publicly demonstrate her receptivity to her future husband's ways.

Driving home from Shelby's wedding, I couldn't help but think about the young woman hurling her shoe out of respect for things Jewish. Certainly her heart was in the right place, but what a sad commentary about the way we seem to be communicating our Jewish heritage to those who are opting to share at least some of it.

I still hold the same concern for the issue of intermarriage and I am no more enlightened and just as befuddled as ever how to deal with those occasions when it becomes inevitable. But that tossing of the shoe to participate in a "Jewish tradition" which was nothing more than silliness, did make one thing perfectly clear: If one wants to bring "Jewishness" into an intermarriage, one ought to do it with the degree of intelligence, sensitivity, and respect to which four thousand years of history is entitled. We owe it at least that much.

Planning an interfaith wedding ceremony, while no doubt facing some hurdles and obstacles, should be viewed as an opportunity to celebrate a beautiful occasion. This is not the place to go into the details which could and have filled books, so what I suggest is that you purchase or peruse one or two of these books as a starting point. Two on the market are: *Celebrating Interfaith Marriages: Creating Your Jewish/Christian Ceremony*, Devon A. Lerner (Holt/Owl), and *Everything Jewish Wedding Book: The Complete Guide to Planning The Ceremony*, which has its own web site at www.netstoreusa.com.

Another web site to visit is Wedding Circle: Jewish Wedding Customs at http:// weddingcircle.com. You might also want to contact The Dovetail Institute for Interfaith Family Resources, which in addition to being very helpful in providing information on the wedding ceremony, furnishes couples in interfaith marriages with educational and networking venues. It also publishes *Dovetail*, a journal for Jewish/Christian families. You may call Dovetail at (800) 530–1596.

So, here we are, having come full circle beginning with our patriarch Abraham, traversing the history of our people, grappling with our own Jewish identity, and now figuring out how we are going to pass all this on so that future generations of Jews will at least be afforded the opportunity of partaking in our great Jewish heritage. Would you want it on your head that after thousands of years of adversity, our generation of Jews will allow to slip through the fingers of time the values we have developed and the special contributions we have made and continue to make? I think not.

If you acquire nothing else from reading this book, I would hope that at the very least you have learned and taken this to heart: Be proud of your Jewish identity! Whatever it is being Jewish may mean to you. In a nutshell, this is the message to convey to your children and grandchildren. Do it with honesty, sincerity, caring, and with an appreciation that others may have a different idea from you regarding exactly how this is done.

After all, isn't this the Jewish way? And for us Jews, what other way can there be?

Afterword

Having been a fan of the popular folk group, Peter, Paul, and Mary, since their first album was released in 1962, it was quite natural that my wife and I took our two sons and went to see the group perform some three decades later. I wanted my sons to hear the music that first moved me so long ago and maintained its sway over me still.

Despite the toll time takes on us frail human creatures, especially on our physical appearances, the melodious voices and warmth of their music was as vibrant as ever, so I was not disappointed. However, I was in for a surprise.

Peter, Paul, and Mary performed one song *that* night, which I never heard them sing before. In fact, despite my collection of Jewish music, what they introduced as a Chanukah song, was new to me. Though Peter Yarrow is Jewish, the group is not known for Jewish music so it is almost as if fate lent a hand that evening and provided me with what would become the final words of this book.

The song is entitled "Light One Candle" and perhaps you have heard it. Obviously, the song has to do with the Jewish Festival of Lights. But what captivates me and is a fitting conclusion to all I have said in these pages, is the third refrain and chorus. If you know the tune sing it aloud and if not, allow the words to pour forth from your heart. These lyrics say it all.

What is the memory that's valued so highly that we keep it alive in that
     flame?
What's the commitment to those who have died when we cry out
     they've not died in vain?
We have come this far always believing that justice will somehow prevail.
This is the burden and this is the promise and this is why we will not fail.

Don't let the Light go out,
It's lasted for so many years.
Don't let the Light go out,
Let is shine through our love and our tears.

Fellow Jews, "Don't let the Light go out."

Appendix

With tens of thousands of books of Jewish interest currently in print and hundreds of new releases each year, it is impossible to provide anything bearing even a representative sample of what is out there to read. But being an avid reader of "Jewish" books and a book reviewer for a number of Jewish periodicals, I hope to present some titles that will at least give you an idea of your options and perhaps pique your interest as to specific books and authors.

A caveat. Like movies, food, and clothing, one's tastes regarding books is highly subjective. Therefore, although I made every effort to present a list of books without regard to my personal preference, I am only human. Hence, the omission of any book or author should not be taken to reflect upon the quality or importance of that work or writer.

You will note that under fiction, I have listed the writer and one or more titles of his or her work. Regarding nonfiction, I placed books in certain categories, which are by no means exhaustive, and as opposed to fiction which is presented in alphabetical order according to the author, here the list is in alphabetical order by title with the exception of Jewish thinkers.

In selecting writers of Jewish fiction, it was not enough that the author be Jewish. There must be more than a scintilla of a Jewish theme present in that writer's work, even if subtle, as with Kafka who was influenced by Yiddish and Zionism. Hence my omission of distinguished writers like Norman Mailer or J.D. Salinger (half Jewish). The same criterion applies to Jewish thinkers—some of their subject matter must be of a Jewish nature.

FICTION

S. Y. Agnon: *The Bridal Canopy*
Aharon Appelfeld: *Badenheim 1939*
Kevin Baker: *Dreamland*
Saul Bellow: *Herzog, Humboldt's Gift*
Nathan Englander: *For the Relief of Unbearable Urges*
Allegra Goodman: *Kaaterskills Falls, The Family Markowitz*
Chaim Grade: *The Sacred and the Profane*
David Grossman: *The Book of Ultimate Grammar*
Joseph Heller: *Good as Gold, Catch 22, God Knows*
Franz Kafka: *The Trial, The Castle, Collected Stories*
Bernard Malamud: *The Fixer, The Tenants, The Assistant*
Amos Oz: *Fima, To Know A Woman*
Cynthia Ozick: *The Shawl, The Puttermesser Papers*
Chaim Potok: *The Chosen, The Promise*
Mordecai Richler: *The Apprenticeship of Duddy Kravitz, Joshua Then and Now, Solomon Gursky Was Here*
Thane Rosenbaum: *Elijah Visible, Second Hand Smoke*
Henry Roth: *Call It Sleep, Mercy of a Rude Stream* (multivolume set)
Phillip Roth: *Portnoy's Complaint, Operation Shylock, I Married A Communist*
Isaac Bashevis Singer: *In My Father's Court, A Crown of Feathers, The Family Moskat, The Manor, Satan in Goray*
I. J. Singer: *The Brothers Ashkenazi*
Leon Uris: *Exodus, Mila 18, Mitla Pass*
Daniel Evan Weiss: *The Swine's Wedding*
Elie Wiesel: *The Fifth Son, A Beggar in Jerusalem, The Oath*
A. B. Yehoshua: *Mr. Mani, A Journey to the End of the Millennium*
Anna Yezierska: *Bread Givers, Salome of the Tenements*

NONFICTION

HOLOCAUST LITERATURE:

Bound Upon A Wheel of Fire, John Dippel.
Hitler's Willing Executioners: Ordinary Germans and the Holocaust, Daniel Goldhagen.
The Holocaust, Leni Yahil.
The Holocaust in American Life, Peter Novick.
I Will Bear Witness, Victor Klemperer.
In Memory's Kitchen: A Legacy from the Women of Terezin, edited by Cara De Silva.
My German Question, Peter Gay.
Night (also *Dawn* and *The Town Beyond the Wall*), Elie Wiesel.
Survival in Auschwitz, Primo Levi.
Theresienstadt, Norbert Troller.
Treblinka, Jean Francois Steiner.
While Six Million Died: A Chronicle of American Apathy, Arthur D. Marie.
The Wiesenthal File, Alan Levy.
Women's Holocaust Writing, Lillian Kremer.
Your Name is Renee: Ruth Kapp Hartz's Story as a Hidden Child in Nazi-Occupied France, Stacy Cretzmeyer.

ISRAEL:

For the Future of Israel, Shimon Peres and Robert Litell.
A History of Israel: From the Rise of Zionism to Our Time, Howard M. Sachar.
Israel: A History, Avner Cohen.
Waging Peace: Israel and the Arabs at the End of the Century, Itamar Rabinovich.
1949: The First Israelis, Tom Segev.

JEWISH COOKBOOKS:

The Book of Jewish Food, Claudia Ruden.
Everyday Cooking for the Jewish Home, Ethel Hoffman.

The Low-Fat Jewish Cookbook, Faye Levy.
A Treasury of Jewish Holiday Baking, Nancy Goldman.

JEWISH HISTORY:

The Gifts of the Jews, Thomas Cahill.
A History of the Jews in America, Abraham Karp.
Jewish Literacy: The Most Important Things to Know About the Jewish Religion, Its People and Its History, Rabbi Joseph Telushin.
The Jewish Time Line Encyclopedia: A Year by Year History from Creation to the Present, Rabbi Mattos Kantor.
Moses: A Life, Jonathon Kirsch.
Why Didn't I Learn This in Hebrew School? Excursion Through the Jewish Past and Present, Eliezer Segal.

JEWISH HOLIDAYS AND OBSERVANCES:

The Kids' Catalog of Jewish Holidays, Jewish Publication Society.
The Book of Jewish Holidays, Ruth Lurie.
Celebrate! The Complete Jewish Holiday Handbook, Lesli Koppelman Ross.
Choosing A Jewish Life, Anita Diamant.
Elijah's Tears: Stories for the Jewish Holidays, (for children), Sydelle Pearl.
Entering the High Holy Days, Reuven Hammer.
Essential Judaism: A Complete Guide to Beliefs, Customs, and Rituals, George Robinson.
Every Person's Guide to Shabbat, Ronald H. Isaacs.
Feast and Festive Meals for the Jewish Holidays, Marlene Soroky, Debbie Shahvar, and Joanne Neuman.
In Every Generation: A Treasury of Inspiration for Passover and the Seder, Rabbi Sidney Greenberg and Pamela Roth.
The Jewish Home: A Guide for Jewish Living, Daniel Syme.
The Jewish Way: Living the Holidays, Irving Greenberg.
On Rosh Hashanah and Yom Kippur, (for children), Cathy Goldberg Fishman.
Queen Esther, The Morning Star (for children), Mordecai Gerstein.
Spiritual Judaism: Restoring the Heart and Soul to Jewish Life, David S. Ariel.

The Tapestry of Jewish Times: A Spiritual Guide to Holidays and Life Cycle Events, Rabbi Nina Beth Cardin.

Trees, Earth and Torah: A Tu B'Shvat Anthology, edited by Ari Elon, Naomi Hyman, and Arthur Waskow.

Understanding Jewish Holidays and Customs, Sol Scharfstein.

1,001 Questions and Answers on Rosh Hashanah and Yom Kippur, Jeffrey Cohen.

JEWISH IDENTITY:

Embracing Judaism: Personal Narratives of Renewed Faith, Debra Gonsher-Vinik.

Exodus to Humanism: Jewish Identity Without Religion, David Ibry.

God-Optional Judaism: Alternatives for Cultural Jews Who Love Their History, Heritage and Community, Judith Seid.

Jew vs. Jew: Inside the Civil Wars of American Jewry, Samuel G. Freedman.

Kaddish, Leon Wieseltier.

Middletown Jews: The Tenuous Survival of an American Jewish Community, edited by Dan Rottenberg.

The Vanishing American Jew, Alan M. Dershowitz.

JEWISH MEN AND WOMEN:

Great Jewish Women, Elinor Slater and Robert Slater.

From Your Father's House: Reflections for Modern Jewish Men, Kerry Olitzky.

On Being A Jewish Feminist, edited by Susannah Heschel.

Searching for My Brothers: Jewish Men in a Gentile World, Rabbi Jeffrey Salkin.

To Be a Jewish Woman, Lisa Aiken.

JEWISH SPIRITUALITY AND MYSTICISM:

Chasidism: Its Development, Theology and Practice, Noson Gurary.

Discovering Jewish Meditation: A Beginner's Guide to an Ancient Spiritual Practice, Nan Fink Gefen.

Every Person's Guide to Death and Dying in the Jewish Tradition, Ronald H. Isaacs.

From Ageing to Sageing (also *Fragments from a Future Scroll*), Zalman Schacter Shalomi.
Hasidism: The Movement and its Masters, Harry M. Rabinowicz.
The Jew in the Lotus, Rodger Kamenetz.
The Jewish Book of Living and Dying, Lewis Solomon.
Jewish Mysticism, Joseph Dan (multivolume work).
Jewish Mysticism: An Anthology, Dan Cohn-Sherbok.
Jewish Views of the Afterlife, Simcha Paull Raphael.
One God Clapping: The Spiritual Path of a Zen Rabbi, Alan Lew with Sherri Jaffe.
Practical Kabbalah: A Guide to Jewish Wisdom for Everyday Life, Laibl Wolf.
Reincarnation in Jewish Thought, Dov Ber Pinson.
Simple Kabbalah, Kim Zetter.
That's Funny You Don't Look Buddhist, Sylvia Boorstein.
These Are My Words: A Vocabulary of Jewish Spiritual Life (also *World of Jewish Spirituality*), Arthur Green.
At the Threshold: Jewish Meditations on Death, edited by Michael Swirsky.

JEWISH THINKERS:

Leo Baeck: *The Essence of Judaism*
Bruno Bettelheim: *Freud's Vienna & Other Essays, Freud & Man's Soul*
Martin Buber: *I and Thou, Tales of the Hasidim, Between Man and Man*
Albert Einstein: *Ideas and Opinions, Out of My Later Years, Essays on Humanism*
Emil L. Fackenheim: *Encounters between Judaism and Modern Philosophy*
Viktor Frankl: *Man's Search For Meaning*
Sigmund Freud: *Moses & Monotheism, Totem & Taboo, The Future of an Illusion*
Abraham Joshua Heschel: *God in Search of Man, Man is Not Alone*
Mordecai Kaplan: *The Meaning of God in Modern Jewish Thought*
Maimonides' Political Thought: Studies in Ethics, Law and the Human Ideal, Howard Kreisel.
Judith Plaskow: *Standing Again at Sinai: Judaism from a Feminist Perspective*

Gershom Scholem: *Major Trends in Jewish Mysticism, Origins of the Kabbalah.* See also *Gershom Scholem: The Man and His Work,* edited by Paul Mendes-Flohr.

Baruch Spinoza: *The Ethics of Spinoza.* See also *Spinoza* by Karl Jaspers.

Jewish Wisdom: Ethical, Spiritual and Historical Lessons from the Great Works and Thinkers, Joseph Telushin.

TRADITIONAL:

The Book of Psalms: A New Translation, M. Rozenberg and M. Zlotowitz.

Broken Tablets: Restoring the Ten Commandments and Ourselves, Rabbi Rachel Mikua.

Ein Yaakov: The Ethical and Inspirational Teachings of the Talmud, Avraham Yoakov Finkel.

Everyman's Talmud, Abraham Cohen.

What Jews Say about God: From Biblical Times to the Present, edited by Alfred J. Kolatch.

A Vocabulary of Jewish Tradition: A Guide to Everyday Practice and Observance, Abraham and Rachel Witty.

YIDDISHKEIT & YIDDISH WRITERS:

Sholom Aleichem: *Some Laughter Some Tears, Old Country Tales*

New Yorkish and Other American Yiddish Stories, edited by Max Rosenfeld.

I. L. Peretz: *Selected Stories*

A Treasury of Sholom Aleichem (children's stories), translated by Aliza Sherrin.

Voices From the Yiddish, edited by Irving Howe and Eliezer Greenberg.

Yiddish Folktales, edited by Beatrice Silverman.

MISCELLANEOUS:

Antisemitism in America, Leonard Dinnerstein.

Becoming a Jewish Parent: How to Add Wonder and Spirituality to Your Child's Life, Daniel Gordis.

The Big Book of Jewish Humor, William Novak and Moshe Waldoks.

The Book of Jewish Values: A Day-by-Day Guide to Ethical Living, Rabbi Joseph Telushin.

A Bintel Brief, Isaac Metzker.

Down to Earth Judaism: Food, Money, Sex and the Rest of Life, Rabbi Arthur Waskow.

The Five Books of Moses for Young People, Esta Cassway.

From Generation to Generation: How to Trace Your Jewish Genealogy and Family History, Arthur Kurzweil.

Haman and the Jews: A Portrait from Rabbinic Literature, Elaine Rose Glickman.

Jewish Music: Its History, People and Song, Ronald Isaacs.

Jewish Renewal, Michael Lerner.

The Satanizing of the Jews, Joel Carmichael.

Torah of the Earth: Exploring 4,000 years of Ecology in Jewish Thought, edited by Arthur Waskow.

Vegetarian Judaism, A Guide for Everyone, Roberta Kalechofsky.

Index

About the Author

Richard D. Bank, an attorney and author, has published numerous articles, essays, book reviews, and short stories in many publications. Except for his first book, *How To Deal With Your Lawyer*, most of his work has been of Jewish interest. He is a past president of the Jewish Children's Folkshul and served as vice-chairman of B'nai B'rith Youth Organization—Philadelphia Region. Richard and his wife, Francine, have two sons and reside in Dresher, Pennsylvania.